KNOWLEDGE-BASED
SPEECH PATTERN
RECOGNITION

KNOWLEDGE~BASED
SPEECH PATTERN
RECOGNITION

Michael Allerhand

Kogan
Page

Acknowledgements

Alex Allerhand, Mavis Barber, Ernie Bate, John Craine, Frank Fallside, Pamela Hinds, Tony Holden, Stephen Levinson, Francis Nolan, Elizabeth Shand, Ian Stanley, Brian Wilson, thank you.

First published 1987 by Kogan Page Ltd
120 Pentonville Road, London N1 9JN

British Library Cataloguing in Publication Data

Allerhand, Michael
    Knowledge-based speech pattern recognition.
    — (Fifth generation computing series).
    1. Automatic speech recognition
    I. Title   II. Series
    006.4'54   TK7882.S65

    ISBN 1 85091 260 2

Printed and bound in Great Britain
by Biddles Ltd, Guildford

621.3819'598
ALL

Contents

CHAPTER 1

Introduction

1.1. Automatic speech recognition as a field of study

Evidently speech recognition is possible; I do it all the time. Assuming the brain is some sort of machine, with the ear and associated organs as a transducer providing an input channel, then it is not beyond the bounds of possibility that the performance of unrestricted recognition of continuous speech could be simulated by computer. Yet after some thirty years of active research, automatic speech recognition (ASR) remains an outstanding problem.

Working in the field of ASR you are forced to accept the inadequacy of current pattern recognition models when measured against the almost boundless sophistication of the human brain. However progress is being made, and though it may take a further thirty years of effort before a machine can be constructed which is capable of comparable performance to a human in this task, the rewards will more than justify the investment.

There are numerous motivations and applications for ASR systems (Martin, 1976; Lea, 1980). Perhaps the greatest benefits will come from a better understanding of human perceptual and cognitive processes. In practice ASR systems will provide a direct channel for communication between the human and the computer; repository of information. This implies a greater understanding of the nature and value of information *per se*, and how this information can be organized.

The field of automatic speech recognition is very wide, encompassing a number of disciplines. The major sources for reference are a number of technical journals; the principal titles are listed as follows.

IEEE Transactions on acoustics speech and signal processing
AT&T Bell systems technical journal
Journal of the acoustical society of America
Speech communication
Cognition
Computer speech and language
IEEE Transactions on pattern analysis and machine intelligence
IEEE Transactions on computers
IEEE Transactions on systems, man, and cybernetics

State-of-the-art reviews appear from time to time, notable examples being Reddy (1976), Klatt (1977), Lea (1980), Mermelstein (1982), Allen *et al.* (1985).

1.2. Why is ASR so difficult?

ASR is difficult, far more so than speech synthesis for example, though this can be seen as a testament to the ability of humans to understand even poorly synthesized speech. The task is basically one of transforming information from one domain of representation into another. This is complicated by the fact that the fundamental nature of the information itself is not clear, and that the principles by which this information is encoded in any representation appear to be extremely complex.

We will consider the speech signal from an engineering point of view as an input to an ASR machine. We will consider a discrete time-varying signal derived from the acoustic signal via an appropriate transducer, and quantized in both time and magnitude for representation inside the digital computer. It will be assumed that the sampling procedures adequately preserve the information in the signal (Rabiner and Schafer, 1978), so that the information is represented in the computer as a sequence of numbers or *samples*, recurring at the sampling rate of the analogue-to-digital conversion. The task of ASR can then be described as one of mapping this numerical representation onto a far more compact symbolic representation, where the symbols represent some abstract categories of linguistic import.

A fundamental requirement of this mapping is that it preserves the contrast between classes of pattern information. For example, a mapping between the acoustic signal and the set of phonemes [1] must preserve the contrast between phonemes. It is an accepted fact that the contrast between particular phonemes is cued by a multiplicity of acoustic features or *correlates*, and it is also evident that different sets of correlates best characterize phonetic contrasts in different phonetic contexts. The uniform use of a single correlate or complex of correlates is generally inadequate. The selection of acoustic correlates, their covariance, and their relationship to context is so very complicated that any direct formulation of the signal-to-symbol mapping appears to be virtually unbounded.

The intuitive approach to this problem is the paradigm known optimistically as *divide and conquer*. According to this paradigm, the problem can be rendered tractable in a piecewise fashion by dividing it into simpler sub-problems which are interrelated in some finite way. The principles by which the domains of speech and language can be usefully sub-divided into simpler domains is an active area of research

---

[1] The phoneme is the basic unit for describing how speech conveys linguistic meaning. A phoneme is a small segment of sound within a word, which is distinguished by its contrast with other such segments. The set of phonemes is a system in which the speech sounds of a language can be classified and represented unambiguously.

in linguistic and cognitive science. The aim of this research is to identify properties of speech and language, based upon inherent constraining influences, which can be used to develop intermediate representational mechanisms, to facilitate the organization of data and the construction of theories. Traditionally the constraint domains have been *acoustic-phonetic* (Fant, 1973), *phonological* (Oshika and Zue, 1975; Zue, 1985), *prosodic* (Lea, 1980), *syntactic* (Woods and Fallside, 1985), *semantic* (Barr and Feigenbaum, 1982), and *pragmatic*.

The application of the divide and conquer strategy based upon these constraint domains is, however, fraught with difficulties. The interrelationships between the constraint domains still appears to be highly complex. Any hard decisions based upon evidence derived in any one domain is likely to conflict in some way with the evidence from another. Each domain contributes partial evidence, which leads to the generation of hypotheses, and every set of hypotheses is of course larger than it need be. In combination, the constraint domains generally compound the number of plausible hypotheses, leading to the characteristic *combinatorial explosion*. Under this effect the number of plausible hypotheses races ahead of the constraints which can be usefully applied to contain them, so that the search problem grows dynamically, producing excessive demands on execution time and memory space.

The constraint domains operate over such a wide scale, that no known inductive procedure can automatically identify the best set of constraints and interrelationships, so as to contain the growth of the set of hypotheses optimally. We shall return to this important point in Chapter 3 where it shall be argued that the structure of these constraint domains need not be entirely *ad hoc*, and can approach a kind of optimality by the application of principled linguistic theory.

To approach unrestricted ASR it is essential to somehow modularize the problem, because there does not appear to be a finite translation scheme from the general speech signal to useful information-bearing symbols. Using the strategy of divide-and-conquer, the acoustic signal is progressively refined through a succession of representational levels, such that the complexity at any given level is contained within reasonable bounds. It is therefore of fundamental importance to consider the selection and the interaction of constraints, paying close attention to the variability of patterns represented at any given level. The ultimate goal is a finite model capable of generating the enormously rich variety of surface phonetic detail in a way that is as deterministic as possible.

1.3. Practical approaches to the problem: two schools of thought

Two distinct schools of thought have been applied to the ASR problem: the *knowledge-based* (KB) approach, and the *pattern recognition* (PR) approach.

Knowledge-based systems are a branch of artificial intelligence which specializes in the building of *expert systems*. In such a system, concepts specific to a particular domain are abstracted as *symbols*, and syntactic or semantic relationships between concepts are defined by *links* between the symbols. The knowledge or expertise of such a system may be formulated as a set of *production rules*, from which any valid structure of symbols and links can be generated by a *search* procedure. This procedure is equivalent to a *parsing* procedure which generates valid sentenial structures from a set of *grammar rules*. In the KB system, *reasoning* is a search procedure, and the program which carries this out is often called an *inference engine*.

The knowledge-based approach, also known as the *rule-based*, or the *computational linguistic* approach, attempts to infer and reproduce the method of ASR based upon the way humans seem to do it. This approach can be traced back to the ARPA speech understanding projects of the early 1970s (Klatt, 1977). Since that time this approach has been actively followed by a number of research groups, principally in academia (Zue, 1985; DeMori, 1983). We could perhaps draw a distinction between the rule-based and the computational linguistic approach if we say that in the latter approach the "strategy" (order of application of knowledge) is implicit in the form of the knowledge (a set of grammatical production rules), while generalized rule-based systems enable strategy to be separated from the knowledge by the provision of scripts, agendas, and so forth (Barr and Feigenbaum, 1982). In this book we will consider only the computational linguistic approach, and when we talk about rules, we mean grammatical production rules.

The pattern-recognition approach is a numerical procedure for the *classification* of *measurement* or *feature vectors*. This classification is based upon a partitioning of the feature space into regions, one region for each *pattern class*. Region boundaries and classification procedures are defined according to some criterion of optimality, which may be based upon geometric, topological, or probabilistic considerations (see Chapter 5).

The pattern-recognition approach, also known as the *pattern-matching* approach, works within a limited constraint domain, and assumes a particular idealization of the speech signal, in order to apply known pattern recognition models which utilize some tractable principle of optimality. The most successful have been approaches based upon template matching (Itakura, 1975; Bridle and Brown, 1979; Rabiner and Levinson 1981), and upon constrained stochastic modelling (Baker, 1975; Jelinek, 1976; Levinson *et al.* 1983). This research has mainly come out of the departments of large companies, the principal companies being IBM and AT&T Bell Laboratories.

It is interesting to consider why these approaches have remained largely independent. The KB approach represents a rather long-term investment. The transfer of specialized knowledge from human expert (linguist or phonetician) to machine is widely regarded as something of a bottleneck.

While complicated data structures such as blackboards [Klatt 1977] offer great flexibility in the application of knowledge and the control of reasoning processes, this complexity works against any tractable principle of optimality. It is difficult to train such complex models since they lack a practical measure by which their convergence onto an optimal model can be observed. Consequently the KB approach is generally not attractive to companies with an interest in ASR. Such companies, which are the source of most of the money for speech research, tend to favour PR approaches. The particular advantage of PR methods is that the parameters which characterize a particular pattern model can be learned automatically from observations of training data. So the use of such methods is almost guaranteed to return some kind of working recognizer, albeit with a relatively restricted performance. This restriction is due to the assumption of *idealized* patterns, generated by a relatively simple pattern model. It is necessary to use a simple pattern model so that the parameter estimation problem is tractable. Nevertheless the restriction to more idealized patterns may be perfectly acceptible in applications which require recognition of speech in some restricted domain, for example the isolated integers. In contrast the KB approach is a research-oriented approach at this time, which has remained in academia by the grace of the various governmental funding agencies. This approach has the far grander goal of unrestricted speech recognition.

There is another reason why the two schools have developed along fairly independent lines, and this concerns the nature of the required expertise. Linguists and computer scientists tend naturally towards a computational linguistic approach, partly because this is their field, and also because their background is not suited to pattern-matching approaches, and they feel uncomfortable in the world of pattern recognition. There are many terminological and ideological differences between these two worlds.

The KB approach leads to models which are intrinsically difficult to describe. Knowledge-based ASR systems are typ-

13

ically described using a lot of words and a lot of rather specialized language. The pattern-matching approach has the advantage in this respect, in that such models can be completely summarized in terms of a few symbolic statements. Such statements are the joy of the mathematician, but the bane of the linguist or phonetician. Research workers with a mathematical or engineering background who favour the PR approach tend to be wary of linguistic approaches. They are generally reluctant to incorporate the wealth of speech and linguistic knowledge, because this would compromise the fundamental optimality principles upon which their pattern-recognition methods are based. Many of them see the addition of such knowledge as the introduction of *ad hoc* rules.

We accept that some symbolic (reasoning) processing is necessary if we are to apply the method of "divide and conquer". However this immediately poses a problem in that we lack a practical measure of the convergence of an evolving system onto an optimal model, in any sense. For highly composite systems, the only globally effective measure is that related to the probability of classification error. In chapter 5 we point out that it is not computationally feasible to use this measure to guide the evolution or training of a highly composite model, and some more practical measures are discussed. This is a real restriction on the sophistication of any rule-based system. We cannot "afford" a very sophisticated knowledge representation and reasoning model, because we cannot ensure it will converge onto any kind of optimality.

In chapter 3 we suggest a reasonable compromise by which the symbolic model is simplified to the point where its performance can be assessed in practice, while still providing a sufficiently rich medium for the expression of linguistic and phonological knowledge. This model maintains a sense of convergence, optimality, and formality while at the same time presenting a friendly environment to the linguist. The basic assumption, which is justified in chapter 3, is that in order to improve the performance of pattern-recognition systems, it is necessary to motivate the choice of constraint, structure, category, and feature from the point of view of linguistic knowledge.

To this end a pattern-recognition machine is developed (see chapter 5) which enables speech knowledge to be incorporated on a direct consultative basis from linguists and phoneticians. The important factors in the specification of this machine are summarized as follows.

1. The rate of knowledge transfer from linguist to computer representation is unimpeded by implementational difficulties.
2. The applied knowledge can be formulated in a principled way, guided by meaningful measures of performance.
3. The model parameters can be estimated automatically from examples of speech training data.
4. The recognition process derives solutions on a basis of maximum likelihood.
5. The model can be formulated and described in a compact way.

The proposed machine is a hybrid which incorporates the advantages of both the knowledge-based and the pattern-recognition approaches. Prior speech knowledge can be represented as a formal qualitative description of speech pattern structure, for which the underlying quantitative properties can be learned automatically from training data. Thus the practical advantage of the PR approach, which is automatic parameterization according to a principle of optimality, is combined with prior knowledge of pattern structure. The result is a richer model which generates a wider variety of speech patterns, with the combinatorial problems contained by the use of principled linguistic theory.

The author wishes to point out that this book does *not* come under the heading of "speech recognition problem solved by revolutionary new techniques in AI knowledge representation and automatic reasoning". The ideas presented in this book are a tentative exploration of the ways in which a simple grammatical representation of the structural constraints inherent in speech and language can be used to improve the descriptive adequacy and the performance of pattern-matching speech recognition models. In this sense, the book is concerned with the representation and application of *a priori* speech knowledge, but the author stresses the fundamental importance of the underlying pattern-matching processes, and the principles of optimality upon which they are based.

1.4. An outline of the chapters to come

Chapter 2 introduces the basis of the hybrid approach, and illustrates it by a simple example of constrained isolated-word recognition. The chapter describes the application of augmented context-free grammar as a representational device, and the use of parametric functions to characterize the underlying quantitative representation.

Chapter 3 argues the case for the introduction of speech-specific knowledge. Parametric and non-parametric methods of speech pattern-recognition are described, and their inherent limitations are discussed.

Chapter 4 deals with the analysis of the speech signal, and the extraction of primitive pattern components. Methods of feature selection and extraction are described. Two novel algorithms are presented for the respective purposes of generating pitch synchronous speech spectrograms, and for segmenting time-evolving spectral energy contours into prominent *events*. The features which are extracted are applied in a real speech recognition task described in Chapter 6.

Chapter 5 begins with a description of the principal methods of numerical pattern classification, to motivate the subsequent description of the hybrid pattern classifier. Estimation procedures for the model parameters are described.

Chapter 6 applies the hybrid machine to the features extracted as described in Chapter 4 in the task of producing a broad-class phonetic transcription of continuous speech input. A structural model of the syllable is developed which incorporates phonotactic and allophonic constraints. The model parameters are estimated from a multi-speaker corpus, and recognition results are given in terms of pattern-class separation. The purpose of this recognizer is to illustrate a well-motivated approach to the formulation of pattern grammars in terms of the hybrid machine, and to generate information on the strength and variability of certain broad phonetic contrasts, based upon a simple set of primitive features.

Chapter 7 concludes the book with some general remarks on the knowledge-based approach to speech pattern recognition, and some suggestions for future work.

During the discussion it will be necessary to involve several pattern recognition methodologies. Where appropriate, the methodology will be briefly reviewed. These reviews are not intended to be exhaustively tutorial; they are required to establish some terminology and define some symbols which will be of subsequent use in the narrative. Where appropriate, references for further study are given.

CHAPTER 2

Recognition of isolated words using feature durations

2.1. Introduction

This chapter is a description of an isolated-word recognizer which illustrates the basis of my approach to the incorporation of speech knowledge into pattern recognition. The isolated-word recognizer discriminates between alternative words in its lexicon using only the order and duration of *voiced*, *voiceless*, and *silence features* [1]. These features have previously been used in a speech training aid for the deaf (Bate *et al*. 1982), where a simple analogue circuit (Knorr, 1979) makes the feature decision from spectral quality and uses this to provide a real-time display.

The display on the monitor screen is a horizontal band, evolving with time, and divided into segments corresponding to voiced, unvoiced, and silent segments. Examples of the display are shown in Figure 2.1. In the figure voiced segments are white, segments of unvoiced frication are chequered, and silent segments are black. The length of each segment is proportional to its duration.

---

[1] Silence is not a distinctive feature in the linguistic sense, but it is extracted as a feature for the purpose of pattern recognition.

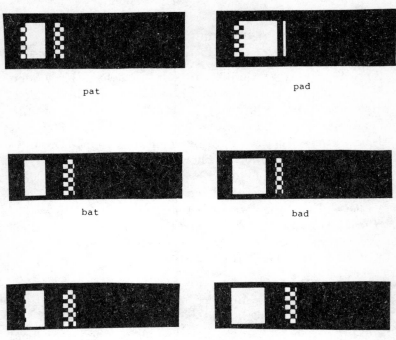

pat

pad

bat

bad

at

art

Figure 2.1. Display of voiced, unvoiced, and silence features

During the work it was found that subjects were able to gauge the length of their own vowel sounds, inaudible to them, from the display. They could also reproduce target patterns corresponding to simple isolated words, thereby learning the complex articulatory switches associated with stop-vowel-stop sequences and so forth. Subjects could also actually read some of the patterns given as targets, and associate particular patterns with particular words. This feat prompted an investigation into the potential of these features for automatic speech recognition. The order and durations of voiced, unvoiced, and silent features have not previously been studied in recognizers, indeed the procedure of dynamic time alignment for template matching actively rejects temporal information.

2.2. Two forms of information

Consider the word "pat". It begins with a release from complete closure at the lips, accompanied by a brief burst of aspiration, and this is followed by the onset and peak of a low front vowel which has inherently short duration, further shortened by the post-vocalic unvoiced stop, which may also be released with a final burst of aspiration. The typical pattern for this word is shown in Figure 2.1. A pattern consisting of silence followed by a brief segment of unvoiced frication, and then a voiced segment, may be observed in a quantity of pattern data to generally correspond to an obstruent. Amongst the obstruents, the classes of voiced stops, unvoiced stops, and affricates may be distinguished by the respective durations of the frication segment.

The contrasts between such categories must be entirely based upon features which can be extracted from the speech signal; in this example a particularly constrained set of features. Further contrasting details emerge when additional features are examined, for instance the spectral quality of the frication segment.

Looking at these patterns it appears that the information they contain is encoded in two essentially different ways: *structurally* (segment order) and *quantitatively* (segment duration). An important difference between these forms of speech information is that while pattern structure is to some extent predictable from intuitions based upon our tacit speech knowledge, the quantitative component is necessarily based upon observations. For example both the pattern which corresponds to an aspirated obstruent and the durational cue to manner of articulation could have been predicted through a simple application of some knowledge of articulatory gestures and their acoustic consequences. Although the durational cue may be qualitatively predictable, in the sense that speech knowledge can provide intuitions about the nature of the correspondence, neither the actual durational differences nor the strength or generality of this contrast are predictable. Such information is defined only in terms of generalizations drawn from observations of data.

2.3. Two forms of pattern recognition

Patterns in which there appears to be a high degree of systematic internal structure are referred to as composite patterns. These patterns are composed of smaller, less complex patterns between which there is a rigid syntactic relationship. The syntax of pattern components is formulated as a set of grammar rules which generatively describe the *language* of such patterns. Constructs of symbolic pattern components are recognized as members of the language by a parsing process. The quantitative component of pattern information is related to the structural component through a signal-to-symbol transformation. Such a transformation is seen as a classification process based upon partitions of a feature or measurement space. The two forms of pattern recognition, referred to as syntactic and vector-space pattern recognition respectively, both have established methodologies and an extensive literature. In order to recognize composite patterns such as speech it is necessary to integrate these two forms of pattern recognition. It appears that this has not been done in automatic speech recognition for grammars more complex than the regular class. This following section describes a simple approach to this problem.

2.4. A model for composite pattern recognition

The proposed model is based upon a context-free description of syllable structure in terms of the features voiced, unvoiced, and silence. A syllabic model is chosen in order to exploit the *phonotactic constraints* [2] upon sequences of intermediate *manner-of-articulation* categories [3]. As has been

---

[2] Phonotactic constraints describe restrictions on the permissable order of phonemes for a given language.

[3] The manner of articulation is a classification of speech sounds based upon the way in which the articulation is accomplished. Manner classes include *vowel, fricative, stop* and so forth.

pointed out by Church (1983), *allophonic variants* [4] can be usefully identified by their position with respect to a syllabic nucleus. In particular, most manner of articulation classes exhibit allophones in word initial and word final positions, for example the aspirated unvoiced stop in word initial contrasts with the glottalized unvoiced stop in word final position ("`tap`"/"`pat`"). The use of a syllabic model enables such allophones to be isolated so that their characterization, in terms of feature order and duration, can be specialized.

Durational rules are incorporated into the grammar by constraining the observed durations at each terminal in a given context using parametric fuzzy subsets. Fuzzy subsets are a simple and intuitive way of partitioning a feature space in order to extract quantitative information. Syntactic pattern recognition is briefly reviewed in the following section in order to define some terminology and symbols which will be used in later chapters. This review is followed by a description of a syntactic pattern recogniser appropriate to the structural information in these simple durational patterns. Then a parametric pattern classifier based upon the idea of fuzzy subsets is described, for the classification of pattern components according to their duration. Finally the composite model is defined with a procedure for evidential reasoning using both structural and quantitative information. Arguments to justify the methods used are reserved until Chapter 3.

2.4.1. Syntactic pattern recognition: a brief review

For syntactic pattern recognition a pattern is represented as a string[5] of pattern primitives, each labelled as a particular *terminal symbol*. If V_t is a set, or alphabet, of terminal symbols then V_t^* denotes the set containing all strings over V_t, including the empty string e. For example

---

[4] Allophonic variants are specific realizations of given phonemes, due to the effect of *coarticulation*, by which the precise articulation of a phoneme is influenced by its immediate context.

[5] Tree and graph grammars (Fu, 1982) will not be discussed.

if $V_t = \{a, b\}$

then $V_t^* = \{e, a, b, aa, ab, ba, bb, aaa, aab, \ldots\}.$

The length of the empty string is zero, denoted $|e| = 0$. Patterns are seen as members of a language over the alphabet V_t. Such a language is a particular subset of V_t^*. For a particular language it may be possible to enumerate all the members of the language, but in general the language is either too large or infinite. The representation of a language can be summarized by denoting certain frequently occurring sub-strings as *non-terminal symbols*, where it is understood that a particular sequence of symbols can be *re-written* for each non-terminal symbol. A hierarchy of such generalizations represents the hidden structure beneath the surface of a language. This structure is formulated in terms of a grammar. Formally a grammar $G = (V_n, V_t, P, S)$, where V_n is a set of non-terminals, V_t a set of terminals, P a set of re-write or *production* rules, and S is the initial symbol. The general form of a production rule is

$$\alpha \rightarrow \beta \qquad (2.1)$$

This rule is interpreted as meaning string β can be written in place of string α in the generative sense. The process of symbol re-writing is called *derivation*. For example if $\delta\alpha\gamma$ is a string, and $\alpha \rightarrow \beta$ is a production, then application of this rule produces the derivation: $\delta\alpha\gamma \Rightarrow \delta\beta\gamma$, ($\delta\alpha\gamma$ derives $\delta\beta\gamma$).

The degree of restriction imposed on the form of the re-write rules is used to classify types of grammar according to the Chomsky hierarchy: *unrestricted, context-sensitive, context-free,* and *regular* (Aho and Ullman, 1972). In general the less restricted the re-write rule, the greater the complexity of the language which can be generated, and the greater the complexity of the parsing process.

The general form of the context-free re-write rule is

$$A \rightarrow \alpha \tag{2.2}$$

where A is restricted to a member of the set of non-terminal symbols, denoted $A \in V_n$, and α is a string of non-terminal and terminal symbols, denoted $\alpha \in \cdot (V_n \cup V_t)^*$. For example Figure 2.2 shows a context-free grammar, the derivation of a particular well-formed pattern, and the corresponding parse tree. This derivation is summarily denoted as $S \overset{*}{\Rightarrow} \alpha$, where α is the string of terminal symbols abcdac, a legal sentence[6] in the pattern language.

The grammar of Figure 2.2 contains a *right recursion* at rule 3. A rule such as $R \rightarrow Rb$ is referred to as *left-recursive*, and a rule such as $R \rightarrow aRb$ is said to be *centre embedded*. Grammatical recursion is the means by which a finite grammar can generate an infinite language.

The grammar of Figure 2.2 is also *non-deterministic*, because at certain stages in the derivation of α there is a choice between more than one possible next direct derivation. A grammar is *ambiguous* when a legal sentence in the pattern language may be derived in more than one way.

The goal of a parsing algorithm is to assess whether or not an input string is grammatical or legal. A sentence is grammatical if there is some derivation that demonstrates that its structure complies with the set of grammar rules. This is a formal procedure analogous to a mathematical proof which demonstrates the truth of an algebraic sentence according to a set of axioms. An additional result of this derivation is a structural account of the input string, in terms of a *parse tree* of non-terminal symbols, rooted at the initial symbol S, with terminal symbols at the leaves of the tree.

---

[6] The use of the word *sentence* is generalized to include string patterns of any kind of named object.

```
1.  S → P, Q.
2.  P → a, R.
3.  R → b, R.
4.  R → c.
5.  Q → d, P.
```

A context-free grammar

```
S → PQ      using rule 1.
  → aRQ     using rule 2.
  → abRQ    using rule 3.
  → abcQ    using rule 4.
  → abcdP   using rule 5.
  → abcdaR  using rule 2.
  → abcdac  using rule 4.
```

Derivation of a legal sentence

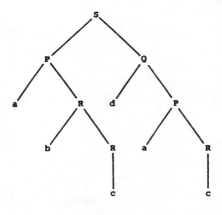

A parse tree

Figure 2.2. (a) Context-free grammar (b) a derivation
(c) parse tree

A parsing algorithm systematically generates all possible derivations until one which matches the input is found, or all possibilities are exhausted. Parsing algorithms vary according to the order in which the productions are applied. The top-down, left-to-right backtracking algorithm is informally described as follows. Starting at the top, with the initial symbol S, generate an initial derivation by applying one rule to re-write S. Thereafter re-write the left-most non-terminal in each successive derivation. This algorithm cannot parse a grammar which contains a left-recursive rule. Clearly the expansion of a left-recursive symbol by re-writing using the same rule will never terminate. The parser generates a succession of *left derivations* of the general form: $xA\beta$, where $x \in V_t^*$, $A \in V_n$, and $\beta \in (V_t \cup V_n)^*$, such as in Figure 2.2. In every derivation, x must match a prefix of the input string, and if this fails the derivation fails. It is not necessary to generate complete strings over the language for comparison with the input. All derivations except the correct one fail before completion.

If the grammar is deterministic, the input is rejected completely as soon as the derivation fails. Non-deterministic grammars provide alternative derivations which can be tried when one fails. The general solution to non-deterministic choice is to try out each alternative derivation in sequence, and *backtrack* to try the next if the derivation fails. Backtracking is the process of returning to a particular place in a derivation, usually the place where the last choice was made, and restoring all variables to their former values. It is conventional to write grammars so that the order in which alternative derivations are tried is explicit in some way. For example in Figure 2.2 rules are applied in simple textual order, so that rule 3 is applied before rule 4, which is applied only if rule 3 fails.

If the grammar is ambiguous it is necessary to introduce some additional criteria to order the alternative successful derivations. One technique, that of stochastic grammar, is discussed in Chapter 5.

For general, context-free grammar the top-down, backtracking parser has an exponential time complexity with respect to the length of the input string (Aho and Ullman, 1972). This is hardly satisfactory, but can be speeded-up in a variety of ways. For example Earleys algorithm (Earley, 1970) has a cubic complexity for the same problem.

Finally a note on grammatical inference. Although it

would be most convenient if a machine could infer a grammar from observations of a set of patterns, such a machine is not available except in certain restricted cases such as regular grammar (Fu and Booth, 1975). In general, inference of context-free grammar cannot be accomplished because the problem of establishing the equivalence of context-free languages is undecidable (Aho and Ullman, 1972). In practice the designer constructs the grammar based on the available pattern knowledge, either manually or interactively.

A comprehensive account of the mathematical properties of formal grammars and parsing algorithms is given by Aho and Ullman (1972). Winograd (1983) provides a summary of natural language understanding by computer. A survey of the applications for syntactic pattern recognition outside the fields of computer and natural languages is given by Fu (1982).

2.4.2. Augmented context-free grammar for structural description

Context-free production rules are the natural way to represent locally embedded structure. However it is often necessary to specify certain contextual dependencies which extend across the bounds of the context-free structure. For example, although vowels and post-vocalic consonants share ancestry in the rhyme of a syllable, it may be convenient to consider their respective derivations as quite independent. In this case additional context dependency is required to represent the durational effect of post-vocalic stops on the vowel. A method for the specification of context dependency is developed in the following paragraphs, which is sufficiently powerful to capture such effects.

The details of this method depend upon the type of parser which is used, and here they are described for the top-down, left-to-right, backtracking parser. For such a parser, a derivation sequence

$$S \Rightarrow \alpha_1 \Rightarrow \cdots \Rightarrow \alpha_i \Rightarrow \cdots \Rightarrow \alpha_n = w \in V_t^*$$

has each $\alpha_i \in (V_n \cup V_t)^*$ of the form $x_i A_i \beta_i$, where $x_i \in V_t^*$, $A_i \in V_n$, and $\beta_i \in (V_n \cup V_t)^*$ (see Figure 2.2).

The context of a non-terminal symbol A_i is described in terms of its *history*, which is contained in the derivation of x_i, and its *expectation*, which is contained in the derivation from β_i. To contain the complexity of specifying and checking context dependency, the history and expectation of a non-terminal symbol is restricted to the immediate context, but includes all the symbols which may exist in this context during the lifetime of the non-terminal.

Let γ be a string $\gamma \in (V_n \cup V_t)^*$, and let $\gamma^{[L]}$ denote its left-most symbol, and $\gamma^{[R]}$ its right-most symbol. The *history* of A_i is defined in terms of the longest derivation sequence

$$\gamma_1 \Rightarrow \cdots \Rightarrow \gamma_m = w \in V_t^*$$

for which $w^{[R]} = x_i^{[R]}$, as the set

$$H(A_i) = \{\gamma_1^{[R]}, \ldots, \gamma_m^{[R]}\}. \tag{2.3}$$

The *expectation* of A_i is defined in terms of the derivation sequence

$$\beta_i \Rightarrow \gamma_1 \Rightarrow \cdots \Rightarrow \gamma_m = w \in V_t^*$$

as the set

28

$$E(A_i) = \{\beta_i^{[L]}, \gamma_1^{[L]}, \ldots, \gamma_m^{[L]}\}. \qquad (2.4)$$

For example, in Figure 2.2, the history of symbol Q is $H(Q) = \{P, R, R, c\}$, and the expectation of symbol P (in the left branch) is $E(P) = \{Q, d\}$.

Given the context of a non-terminal symbol in terms of its history and expectation, a context dependency can be specified as follows. A context-free production rule $A \to \alpha$ is optionally allowed the extra notation

$$[A_1]A[A_2] \to \alpha \qquad (2.5)$$

where $A_1, A_2 \in (V_n \cup V_t)$, A_1 is a left-context dependency, and A_2 a right-context dependency for the non-terminal symbol A. The context is then restricted using the conditions

$$A_1 \in H(A) \text{ and } A_2 \in E(A). \qquad (2.6)$$

We will now see how the history and expectation sets for each non-terminal symbol can be calculated on-the-fly during a parse, and how a specific context dependency is checked.

In a left-to-right parse, history sets $H(A)$ are initialized at each terminal substring, and accumulate during the parse. Left-context dependency is checked at each non-terminal so that $A_1 \in H(A)$.

The expectation sets are unknown, but the symbols for right-context dependency, A_2, can be accumulated during the parse in an expected-symbol set $e(A)$. If each symbol which could be in the expectation set $E(A)$ is deleted from $e(A)$ when it appears, then we can check right-context dependency using the fact that all the expected symbols in $e(A)$ should have been deleted by the time a terminal substring is reached. The expected symbols will be *consumed* by a parse which satisfies the right-context dependencies.

When a left-context check fails at a rule, or when the expected symbol set $e(A)$ is not entirely consumed at a terminal, the parser is forced to backtrack until it can find a parse which satisfies all the left and right context dependencies.

These conditions are met procedurally in the following four clauses which apply to each production rule. Initially $H(A) = \emptyset$ and $e(A) = \emptyset$. Consider the parse at an intermediate stage when the derived string is $xA\beta$, and the production rule $[A_1]A[A_2] \rightarrow \alpha$ is applied. The current history and expected-symbol set are $H(A)$ and $e(A)$ respectively. Context dependency is checked upon application of the rule. Upon successful completion of the rule, new sets $H(B)$ and $e(B)$ are calculated, and these are the history and expected-symbol sets of the next symbol, $B = \beta^{[L]}$.

Upon application of a rule:

1. Consume expected symbol.
   a. Delete every A in $e(A)$.
   b. If $\alpha^{[L]} \in V_t$ then delete every $\alpha^{[L]}$ in $e(A)$.
2. Check context dependency.
   a. Test $A_1 \in H(A)$.
   b. If $\alpha \in V_t^*$ then test $e(A) = \emptyset$.

Upon successful completion of the rule:

3. If $\alpha \in V_t^*$ then $H(B) = \{A, \alpha^{[R]}\}$
      else $H(B) = \{A\} \cup H(A)$.
4. $e(B) = e(A) \cup \{A_2\}$.

In clause 1, all occurrences of the leftmost symbol are deleted so that clause 2 can handle right-recursive rules which generate expectation, for example $R[d] \rightarrow b, R$. When the parser backtracks, the H and e sets must be restored to their former states at the point to which the parser returns. This process is delegated to the backtracking mechanism, which records the H and e sets along with other information for the purpose of re-instantiation on backtracking.

This context dependency is limited to adjacent symbols, but these symbols can be any of the symbols derived between a common ancestor and the terminals. Therefore the dependency extends to restrict the derivations of the common ancestor. The specification of context dependency described here differs from other approaches, notably Generalized Phrase Structure Grammar (Gazdar, 1982) and Definite Clause Grammar (Periera and Warren, 1977). In these approaches, contextual information is propagated by structures which contain the values of specific feature attributes. These attributes are an abstraction of some property of the associated syntactic category. In the method described above, the contextual information consists of category names, but the range over which contextual dependencies may operate is extended. In this way specification of context dependency is closely related to the grammatical alphabets, in the manner of a bounded context sensitivity.

2.4.3. Parametric fuzzy subsets: a brief review

The idea of a parametric restriction on a feature is developed in this example using the idea of fuzzy subsets (Zadeh, 1975). A universe of discourse W is the set of all duration measures. If A is a finite subset of W, whose elements are $w_1, \ldots, w_n$, then A may be expressed as the union of singletons

$$A = w_1 + \cdots + w_n. \qquad (2.7)$$

This notation is extended to express the finite fuzzy subset F_A of W as:

$$F_A = \chi_1/w_1 + \cdots + \chi_n/w_n \qquad (2.8)$$

where χ_i is the grade of membership of w_i in F_A, and is a real number in the interval $[0,1]$, with 0 indicating no membership and 1 indicating full membership.

The fuzzy subset is a union of fuzzy singletons which may expressed as an integral

$$F_A = \int_W \chi_A(w)/w \qquad (2.9)$$

in which $\chi_A : W \to [0,1]$ is called the membership function of the fuzzy subset F_A.

In the case where W is a set of measurements such as duration, it is convenient to express the membership function of a fuzzy subset of the real numbers in terms of a parametric function. One such function of the form shown in Figure 2.3 is defined below.

$$
\begin{aligned}
S(w; \alpha, \beta, \gamma, \delta) &= 0 & , & \quad w \leq \alpha, w \geq \delta \\
&= 1 & , & \quad w \geq \beta, w \leq \gamma \\
&= 2 \left(\frac{w-\alpha}{\beta-\alpha} \right)^2 & , & \quad \alpha \leq w \leq \frac{\alpha+\beta}{2} \\
&= 1 - 2 \left(\frac{\beta-w}{\beta-\alpha} \right)^2 & , & \quad \frac{\alpha+\beta}{2} \leq w \leq \beta \qquad (2.10) \\
&= 1 - 2 \left(\frac{w-\gamma}{\delta-\gamma} \right)^2 & , & \quad \gamma \leq w \leq \frac{\gamma+\delta}{2} \\
&= 2 \left(\frac{\delta-w}{\delta-\gamma} \right)^2 & , & \quad \frac{\gamma+\delta}{2} \leq w \leq \delta.
\end{aligned}
$$

The function $\chi_A(w) = S_A(w; \alpha, \beta, \gamma, \delta)$ is the grade of membership of feature w in F_A, defined by the parameters $\alpha, \beta, \gamma, \delta$. For example if $F_A = $ short, then the function expresses a degree of belief that w is a short segment.

The operations of union and intersection of fuzzy subsets F_A and F_B are defined by:

$$F_A \cup F_B = \int_W \chi_A(w) \vee \chi_B(w)/w \qquad (2.11)$$

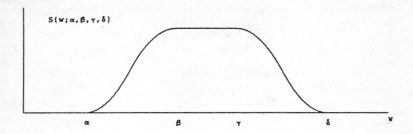

Figure 2.3. Fuzzy-set membership function

$$F_A \cap F_B = \int\limits_W \chi_A(w) \wedge \chi_B(w)/w \qquad (2.12)$$

where $\vee$ and $\wedge$ denote the operators max and min respectively. The complement of F_A is defined by

$$F'_A = \int\limits_W \left(1 - \chi_A(w)\right)/w. \qquad (2.13)$$

For example if $F_A = \textbf{short}$ and $F_B = \textbf{long}$, then the degree of belief that w_1 is a short segment and w_2 is a long segment is

$$\chi_A(w_1) \wedge \chi_B(w_2). \qquad (2.14)$$

The degree of belief that w_1 is not short is

$$1 - \chi_A(w_1). \qquad (2.15)$$

An introduction to the theory of fuzzy subsets is provided by Zadeh (1975). A survey of the application of fuzzy sets to pattern recognition is given by Kandell (1982). For fuzzy set

33

theory and speech recognition, see DeMori (1984), and also Pal and Majumdar (1977).

2.4.4. A composite model

The model parameters are the context-free grammar and the fuzzy-set membership functions. The grammar $G = (V_n, V_t, P, S)$ where V_n is a set of non-terminal symbols, V_t is a set of terminal symbols $V_t = \{T_v, T_u, T_s\}$ for voiced, unvoiced, and silence categories, P is a set of production rules, and S is the initial symbol. A production rule in P has the general form $[A_1]A[A_2] \rightarrow \alpha$, where $A \in V_n$, $\alpha \in (V_n \cup V_t)^*$, and $A_1, A_2 \in (V_n \cup V_t)$ are optional context dependency specifiers.

The input patterns are a sequence of observations $\mathbf{O} = O_1, \ldots, O_i, \ldots, O_n$ where O_i is a symbol in V_t and $f(O_i)$ is the duration measurement associated with O_i.

The numerical duration measurement associated with each terminal symbol is given a qualitative linguistic description using the idea of fuzzy sets. Each terminal symbol $T_k \in V_t$ is associated with an alphabet of fuzzy sets

$$\{F_{1k}, F_{2k}, \ldots, F_{jk}, \ldots\} \qquad (2.16)$$

providing a range of fuzzy restrictions on the duration measurement associated with T_k. A particular restriction defines a particular *class* of duration pattern. This class is defined *quantitatively*, or numerically, through the membership function of a fuzzy set F_{jk}, and is denoted in the grammar as $(j)T_k$, where the symbol j is a *qualitative* description of this class in terms of the feature duration.

For example, a grammatical notation '(short)voiced' describes a terminal symbol 'voiced' which has a fuzzy restriction 'short' on the associated duration observation. This restriction is one of a set, such as {'short', 'medium', 'long', ...} which apply to duration observations associated with this symbol. The symbol 'short' is a qualitative description of the structural component 'voiced', in terms of feature duration.

Each fuzzy set F_{jk} is described by a membership function χ_{jk} such as (2.10), and characterized by particular values of the parameters α, β, γ, and δ. A procedure of *parameter estimation* from observations of training data identifies the parameters of the fuzzy set membership functions. In this way the model learns the relationship between the symbolic, qualitative description of patterns given in the grammar, and their underlying numerical properties found in the data.

The goal of this learning process is to maximize the performance of the model. Here we shall not consider learning processes which continue indefinitely, but we shall use a supervised learning approach which aims to maximize the *degree of belief* in each of a set of known training patterns. This approach is based upon the principle of maximum likelihood, which informally states that if the performance of the model, in terms of some measure of the pattern-to-class match, is optimized for a set of known patterns, then the model is most likely to make the correct decisions for unknown patterns.

The degree of belief in a pattern is the value of the combined evidence which results from the pattern. We will now derive a *decision rule* which combines evidence from each observation in a sequence of observations, to classify a sequential pattern. The rule produces a value for the combined evidence which can then be maximized as the objective of the parameter estimation procedure.

In the string of terminals $w = w_1, \ldots, w_i, \ldots, w_n$, the degree of belief, or likelihood in the fuzzy sense, for a terminal symbol $w_i = (j)T_k$, given an observed symbol O_i with duration $f(O_i)$, is the grade of membership of $f(O_i)$ in the fuzzy set F_{jk}. This is expressed in terms of the fuzzy set membership function χ_{jk} as follows:

$$
\begin{aligned}
\text{bel}(w_i/O_i) &= \chi_{jk}\big(f(O_i)\big), & T_k &= O_i \\
&= 1 &, \quad T_k &= O_i, \; j = \emptyset \qquad (2.17) \\
&= 0 &, \quad T_k &\neq O_i
\end{aligned}
$$

where $j = \emptyset$ is to denote zero fuzzy restriction on the measurement.

The degree of belief in a string w, conditioned on a sequence of observations O, is the logical intersection of the degree of belief in each terminal w_i, given observation O_i.

$$
\text{bel}(w/O) = \bigcap_{i=1}^{n} \text{bel}(w_i/O_i) \qquad (2.18)
$$

If the grammar is ambiguous, and can generate m distinct derivations of w, where the terminals have different fuzzy restrictions, then

$$
\text{bel}(w/O) = \bigcup_{m} \bigcap_{i=1}^{n} \text{bel}(w_i/O_i) \qquad (2.19)
$$

Since the belief functions are defined as fuzzy sets, (2.19) is expressed using (2.11) and (2.12)

$$
\text{bel}(w/O) = \bigvee_{m} \bigwedge_{i=1}^{n} \text{bel}(w_i/O_i) \qquad (2.20)
$$

This formula describes the composition of evidence grades. The objective of the parser is now to derive string w which maximizes $\text{bel}(w/O)$. Given the input string O, the string w then represents the derivation in which the model has the highest degree of belief, because it is supported by the maximum evidence.

An additional advantage of the *max-min decision rule* (2.20) is that an exhaustive parse is not necessarily essential. For two derivations $y \in V_t^*$ and $z \in V_t^*$ it follows from (2.20) that

$$\text{bel}(y/\mathbf{O}) < \text{bel}(z/\mathbf{O}) \qquad (2.21)$$

if there exists $1 \leq i \leq n$ such that
$$\text{bel}(y_i/\mathbf{O}_i) < \text{bel}(z/\mathbf{O})$$

It is therefore admissible to evaluate (2.20) without having to parse m complete derivations. A derivation fails as soon as any component membership grade falls below the current max $\text{bel}(w/\mathbf{O})$.

A grammar may be written which is a qualitative description of syllabic structure in terms of voiced, unvoiced, and silence features and the associated duration constraints. Qualitative descriptions of durational effects are predictable in the sense that certain contrasts, for example 'short'/'long', are predictable in certain contexts according to phonological knowledge. The quantitative constraints on durations are derived from particular fuzzy subsets which are *trained* on observations of data. In this simple one-dimensional case the membership function parameters can be estimated by hand from observation of the feature clusters, so as to maximize (2.20) for $w = \mathbf{O}$ over all strings $\mathbf{O}$ in the training data. Methods for automatic parameter estimation are described in Chapter 5.

2.5. Constrained recognizer using feature durations

The recognizer is based upon a syntactic model of syllables in isolated words. Strings of features are parsed into manner-of-articulation classes, which are subsequently used to access words in the lexicon. Weighting criteria between alternative syllabic derivations is obtained from inherent class durations, and context dependent durational rules. In particular each class is described by a conjunction of fuzzy variables, and derivations are ranked according to their composite degree of belief, obtained from the appropriate fuzzy-set membership functions. The knowledge of the system is then incorporated in the definition of the grammar, and the assignment of the membership functions. An important part of the approach adopted is that it can be readily augmented to include features in addition to duration, such as vowel and fricative quality and pitch, as additional attributes rather than a complete re-write of the recognizer rules.

2.5.1. Syllabic model

The grammar of Figure 2.4 shows the syllabic model. This grammar is used to parse strings of features into manner of articulation classes. Strings of these classes are matched with strings in the lexicon to access particular words. Alternatively the grammar can be driven by particular words, for example the rule

`pat → init_uv_stop, short_vowel, final_uv_stop.`

derives the feature string UVSU.

The range of manner classes is representative but not exhaustive; nasals and liquids are not considered in order to avoid undefinable class boundaries, in terms of the features used. Alternative feature strings are provided to describe, for example, the possibility that an initial vowel may have a glottal onset (as in 'art) , devoicing of final consonants, and de-aspiration of final stops. The feature extraction provides no measure of voice onset time, except that which can be derived from burst duration.

Recall from the model definition (2.17) that a terminal such as (h1)U consists of a symbol U, and a reference to a fuzzy-set membership function h1, which is one of the set of durational constraints (2.16) on the category U. In a declarative interpretation of this terminal the symbol h1 is a qualitative description of the structural component U, in terms of the

```
word → syl.
word → init_syl, final_syl.

syl → init_cons, vowel, final_cons.
syl → init_vowel, final_cons.

init_syl → init_cons, vowel.
init_syl → vowel.

final_syl → medial_cons, vowel, final_cons.

init_cons → init_vstop.
init_cons → init_uvstop.
init_cons → init_vfric.
init_cons → init_uvfric.
init_cons → init_affric.

init_vowel → U, vowel.
init_vowel → vowel.

vowel → long_vowel.
vowel → short_vowel.

medial_cons → vstop.
medial_cons → uvstop.

final_cons → final_vstop.
final_cons → final_uvstop.

init_vstop → Ø.
init_uvstop → (short_burst)U.
init_vfric → Ø.
init_uvfric → (long_burst)U.
init_affric → (med_burst)U.

long_vowel[vstop] → (lengthened_long)V.
long_vowel[uvstop] → (shortened_long)V.

short_vowel[vstop] → (lengthened_short)V.
short_vowel[uvstop] → (shortened_short)V.

vstop → (very_short)S.
uvstop → (quite_short)S, (short_burst)U.

final_vstop → (very_short)S, (short)V.
final_vstop → Ø.

final_uvstop → (quite_short)S, (very_short_burst)U.
final_uvstop → Ø.
```

Figure 2.4. Isolated word grammar using feature durations

feature duration. In parameter estimation the model learns an underlying quantitative description of U from observations of training data.

A rule such as long_vowel[v_stop] → (h4)V specifies a local context dependency. The symbol 'v_stop' is expected in the right context of long_vowel, as defined in section 2.4.2. This rule describes an allophonic effect in which the vowel duration is *lengthened* by the following voiced stop. Given the context, the symbol **h4** describes the appropriate durational constraint on the vowel.

A list of durational effects known to convey linguistic information has been provided by Klatt (1976), and these effects are the basis for the durational rules. The proposed rules use inherent phonological durations (short/long vowels, voiced/voiceless fricatives, voice onset times) the influence of a post-vocalic consonant on vowel duration (voiced/voiceless contrast) and word boundary effects (vowel lengthening in word final syllable).

The recognition is constrained in that only those feature strings which exhibit the appropriate contrasts in feature order and duration can be discriminated. The purpose of this recognizer is to generate information on the type and strength of these contrasts, and in what ways they are affected by inter- and intra-speaker variation. This was achieved by training the recognizer on appropriate pairs of maximally and minimally contrasting words, from a variety of speakers. Initially a lexicon of 27 words was chosen which illustrate maximal and minimal contrasts in terms of the proposed durational rules. Three speakers (a woman and two men) read the lexicon in random order to generate training and test data.

The grammar is written in PROLOG (Warren and Pereira, 1977), a language having many parallels with LISP, but seeming especially attractive in this application because grammar production rules can be written (with a little extra syntax) directly as program statements. These statements are then interpreted by the PROLOG theorem-proving search, which is entirely equivalent to a top-down, left-to-right, backtracking parser. This is not the most efficient way to parse context-free grammar; the search has exponential complexity in general (Aho and Ullman, 1972). However the interest in this work is concerned with models and methodology rather than implementation details, and certain other

	add	bad	pad	fad	bard	adder	padded	patted	batted	part	art	at	bat	pat	vat	fat	chat	sat
add	66	66	66															
bad	97	97	97		86													
pad	100	100	100															
fad	100	100	100	100	70													
bard	60	60	60	60	70													
adder						43												
padded							50											
patted							22	82	82									
batted								56	56									
part										100	100							
art											72	72	72	72	72	72		
at												100		100	100			
bat											87	87	100	100	100	100		
pat												100	100	100	100			
vat											87	87	100	100	100	100		
fat											50	82	100	50	50	66	100	
chat																	100	
sat																		100

Figure 2.5. Confusion matrix of isolated word recognition results

facets of PROLOG which make implementation particularly easy outweigh the complexity disadvantage. In particular the restoration of previous instances of variables or structures during backtracking is transparently automated by the PROLOG interpreter. Program statements, or clauses, are remarkably free of distracting detail and are highly declarative, which aids their comprehensibility and their correctness in general.

2.5.2. Results

Recognition results for the test data using the model estimated on the training data are shown in Figure 2.5 as a

41

confusion matrix. In the figure the rows are the input words, and the columns are the words for which the model found a significant degree of belief. This is expressed as a percentage of complete belief. There was considerable inter-and intra-speaker variation in the durational patterns, but contrasts due to certain durational rules appear to be strong In particular the two clusters of results in Figure 2.5 illustrate the distinctive contrast between vowel/voiced-stop and vowel/voiceless-stop pairs (e.g. 'pad'/'pat'). This is due to a combination of shortening/lengthening rules for vowels under the influence of following stops, and the inherent durations of stops and bursts for voiced and voiceless stops. Across all three speakers, short vowels preceding voiceless stops show a duration of voicing between 70 and 180 mS, short vowels preceding voiced stops and long vowels preceding voiceless stops show a duration 170–280 mS, and long vowels preceding voiced stops show a duration 260–330 mS. Burst duration for voiced stops is 0–35 mS, and for voiceless stops is 30–70 mS. Certain contrasts which are difficult to detect by other methods, for example 'pat'/'part', are quite distinct. The use of burst duration exclusively is unreliable, as final voiced stops are often un-released (e.g. 'pad'), however the duration of the stop is also informative, being 30–70 mS for voiced stops, and 60–120 mS for voiceless stops. Voiceless fricatives and affricates are distinctive, the duration of voiceless frication of initial 'f', 'ch', and 's' being respectively 20–40 mS, 50–90 mS, and 110–160 mS. It is difficult to distinguish between initial stops which are only weakly aspirated, and furthermore there is confusion with initial vowels, which may be strongly glottalized. This is illustrated by each cluster in Figure 2.5. Performance here could have been improved by including /AE/ before each word, as in 'a pat'. With bi-syllabic words there is real difficulty unless the stop between syllables is clear, and this is not completely reliable. In the absence of stress, vowels in word initial syllables are some 15% shorter than in word final or monosyllables.

2.6. Conclusions

Feature durations are a relatively speaker independent cue for discrimination of vowel-stop pairs, short/long vowels, and voiceless fricatives. Contrasts described by durational rules concerning inherent phonological durations, the influence of a post-vocalic consonant on vowel duration, and word boundary effects, are strong. Durational information is most reliable at small-scale events, such as stops and bursts. Over larger scales such as vowel durations, the effects of articulation rate become an important factor. In this experiment the articulation rate was kept fairly constant, and this probably contributed to the success of distinctions like 'pat'/'part'. As has been pointed out by Stevens and Blumstein (1981), vowel durations cannot in general be regarded as an invariant cue. However they are not useless; inherently short vowels are distinct with some invariance to speaker and articulation rate.

The use of parametric fuzzy subsets to constrain durations leads to a very simple parametric model. The decision rule, which is based upon the max-min rule of fuzzy logic, is a *weak* rule in the sense that it grades derivations pessimistically according to their lowest-scoring component. Each derivation is therefore dependent upon the weakest link in the chain. However, provided the quantitative pattern classes are sufficiently distinct, as seems to be the case, then this rule is quite adequate. The concept of fuzzy variables applies well to the inherent vagueness of feature durations, the evaluation and composition of belief values is arithmetically simple, and the resulting hypotheses, though themselves fuzzy by definition, are sufficient for purposes of discrimination.

The recognizer derives its power from its ability to use both structural and quantitative information at the feature level. The structural theory provides contextual constraints. These constraints serve to isolate particular categories for which the observed durations form distinct clusters which can be characterized by parametric membership functions. Context-dependent durational effects can be described using a combination of both structural and quantitative information.

An important part of the feature-based strategy for speech recognition, which is not illustrated in this chapter, is the selection of appropriate feature complexes to cue particular speech categories. It is well-known that judicious choice of feature complexes, the intersection of two or more features, increases class separation and the contrast between speech categories. Feature selection and extraction is discussed in Chapter 4.

CHAPTER 3
Speech pattern recognition

3.1. Introduction

The isolated word recognizer presented in the last chapter is a very simple parametric model, where the parameters are the context-free grammar and the fuzzy-set membership functions. The grammar was not inferred, but specified. The membership functions were estimated from observations of training data. The model illustrates the inter-dependence of two forms of information, quantitative and structural, and this theme is expanded in this chapter.

The two most successful pattern recognition models which have been applied to ASR, template matching and hidden Markov models, are described and discussed. These models are necessarily relatively simple so that the parameter estimation procedures are tractable. However the use of simple models creates an inherent performance limitation; a plateau is reached and further improvement cannot be made. Basically these simple models are just not rich enough to describe a process as specialized as speech recognition.

Models of sufficient detail cannot be inferred from observations of speech data alone. The required inference procedures are not known, and in any case humans make use of a variety of other kinds of observations when learning to recognize speech. A practical solution to the problem is to incorporate top-down linguistic knowledge. It is argued that prior knowledge of language and speech should motivate sequential decision processes and pattern classification, in order to improve upon the *local* optimality of recognition models based upon maximum likelihood estimation, such as templates and hidden Markov models.

3.2. Models for speech pattern recognition

Amongst the themes common to the more successful speech recognizers of recent years, the most influential has been the adaptation of well-founded optimality principles. This optimality is possible by casting the problem in such a way that composite measures of likelihood can be maximized.

The theme of likelihood, which is identified (Levinson, 1985b) as the common Baysian foundation upon which all these methods rest, may derive from class-conditional probability density functions or stochastic models in the case of parametric methods such as hidden Markov models (HMMs), or may derive from distance functions in the case of nonparametric methods such as template matching.

3.2.1. Template matching

In template matching methods the decision-making process matches the unknown input to each of a set of templates, which are prototype examples of pattern data. The matching criterion is generally a correlation which directly reflects the similarity between input and template. The use of whole-word templates has achieved quite a measure of success, largely due to the procedure of dynamic time alignment (Bridle and Brown, 1979) of input and template, which provides a degree of normalization for the intra-class temporal variations. First we shall discuss linear prediction analysis of the speech signal, which will lead us to the Itakura metric, a measure of similarity between a test pattern and a reference pattern. Then we discuss the dynamic programming technique for optimally aligning the test and reference patterns for comparison and matching.

Linear prediction (LP) analysis has been a widely used method for producing a parametric representation of the speech signal since the early 1970s (Markel and Gray, 1976). We assume that the speech signal can be adequately modelled by a linear filter, driven by periodic impulses (for voiced speech) or by white noise (for unvoiced speech), and we estimate the parameters of this filter using the method of least squares.

The general m-order linear difference equation for sampled data describes the input-output characteristics of the filter

$$
\begin{aligned}
s(k) + a_1 s(k-1) + \cdots + a_m s(k-m) = \\
b_0 u(k) + b_1 u(k-1) + \cdots + b_n u(k-n)
\end{aligned}
\tag{3.1}
$$

with $a_0 = 1$. At time $t = k$ the output sample is $s(k)$, and the driving sample is $u(k)$.

$$
s(k) = -\sum_{i=1}^{m} a_i s(k-i) + \sum_{i=0}^{n} b_i u(k-i)
\tag{3.2}
$$

Taking the Z-transform we find

$$
S(z) = -\sum_{i=1}^{m} a_i z^{-i} S(z) + \sum_{i=0}^{n} b_i z^{-i} U(z)
\tag{3.3}
$$

from which the transfer function of the filter is

$$
H(z) = \frac{S(z)}{U(z)} = \frac{\sum_{i=0}^{n} b_i z^{-i}}{1 + \sum_{i=1}^{m} a_i z^{-i}}
\tag{3.4}
$$

In practice it has been found that a good approximation to the vocal tract filter is the all-pole model, with order around $m = 12$.

$$H(z) = \frac{G}{1 + \sum_{i=1}^{m} a_i z^{-i}} \tag{3.5}$$

where G is a gain factor which we shall subsequently ignore. Here the zeroes in the numerator of (3.4) are removed. Such as step is reasonable since zeroes only contribute to the modelling of nasal sounds [1], by modelling the effect of cancellation due to the coupling with the nasal cavity. In the sample domain this transfer function describes an m-order autoregressive process in which a *predicted* ouput is defined in terms of a weighted sum of past outputs.

$$\hat{s}(k) = -\sum_{i=1}^{m} a_i s(k - i) \tag{3.6}$$

To identify this filter we wish to estimate the parameters a_i to minimize the squared error between this predicted output and the actual output. Consider the inverse filter of (3.5)

$$H^{-1}(z) = 1 + \sum_{i=1}^{m} a_i z^{-i} \tag{3.7}$$

In the sample domain we have

$$u(k) = s(k) + \sum_{i=1}^{m} a_i s(k - i) \tag{3.8}$$

From (3.6) we see that $u(k)$ represents a residual prediction error.

---

[1] Recent work has demonstrated an improvement in the modelling of nasal sounds using a pole-zero model and recursive estimation techniques such as Kalman filtering (Morikawa H. Fujisaki H. "System Identification of the Speech Production Process Based on a State-Space Representation." *IEEE Trans* ASSP-32 252-262 1984).

$$u(k) = s(k) - \hat{s}(k) \qquad (3.9)$$

The familiar idea of least-squares estimation is used to estimate the predictor coefficients. We calculate the coefficients a_i which minimize the total squared predictor error over a sequence of N samples. We find a_i such that

$$e = \sum_N u(k)^2 = \sum_N \left(s(k) + \sum_{i=1}^{m} a_i s(k - i) \right)^2 \qquad (3.10)$$

is minimized. We must assume the signal remains stationary over the N samples so that the filter may have constant coefficients [2]. The minimization procedure is detailed by Markel and Gray (1976). We first differentiate (3.10) to get the normal equations $\partial e / \partial a_i = 0$, which are a set of m equations in m unknowns, and then these are solved simultaneously to arrive at the estimates of the predictor coefficients. The principal methods of solution, the autocorrelation method, the covariance method, and the lattice method, are also described by Rabiner and Schafer (1978).

The Itakura metric [3] is a measure of the similarity between a test pattern and a reference pattern. It is the log ratio of the minimum total squared predictor errors of the reference and test patterns. Writing (3.10) as

---

[2] Speech is clearly a non-stationary signal, but it can be modelled by a time-invariant filter under the assumption of short-time stationarity. That is, that speech is a concatenation of fairly stationary segments of around 10mS or so. This is due to the physical constraints on the speed at which the vocal tract can change shape.

[3] A metric is a generalized distance measure which obeys certain axioms of Euclidean distance, in particular a metric distance is non-negative and is the shortest distance between two points in a metric space.

$$e = \sum_N \left(\sum_{i=0}^m a_i s(k - i) \right)^2 \qquad (3.11)$$

we have

$$e = \sum_{i=0}^m \sum_{j=0}^m \left(a_i a_j \sum_N s(k - i)s(k - j) \right) \qquad (3.12)$$

Now by defining an autocorrelation matrix $R_{ij} = \sum_N s(k - i)s(k - j)$ we can write the sum of square errors as

$$e = \sum_{i=0}^m \sum_{j=0}^m a_i a_j R_{ij} \qquad (3.13)$$

and in vector notation

$$e = a^t R a \qquad (3.14)$$

If the LP coefficients of the test pattern are denoted a_T, and those of the reference pattern a_R, then the Itakura metric is defined [4]:

$$d(T, R) = \log \frac{a_R^t R a_R}{a_T^t R a_T} \qquad (3.15)$$

An efficient method for computing this distance is given by Itakura (1975).

---

[4] The metric (3.15) is known as a *log likelihood ratio* because the quadratic forms essentially describe the covariance of the probability distribution of the parameters a (Rabiner and Schafer, 1978).

The technique of dynamic time alignment minimizes the Itakura distance between an input speech pattern and a reference template. Both test and reference patterns are divided into a sequence of short stretches of signal called frames for short-time LP analysis. Factors affecting the choice of frame size are discussed in Chapter 4. The distance between test and reference patterns is calculated per frame, but this local distance is subject to variations due to the differences between the rate at which people speak. For a test pattern of N frames, $1 \leq n \leq N$, and a reference pattern of M frames $1 \leq m \leq M$, the time alignment procedure obtains the optimal alignment function $m = w(n)$ such that the global distance between test and reference is minimized. The distance between test and reference patterns is then

$$D = \min_{w(n)} \sum_{n=1}^{N} d\big(n, w(n)\big) \qquad (3.16)$$

where $d(n, m)$ is the local frame-to-frame distance from the Itakura metric (3.15). Variations in local pattern structure are accounted for by minimising the test-to-reference distance over all possible alignments, subject to certain variational constraints. If all the possible alignments of N test frames and M reference frames are seen as paths through an $N \times M$ grid, then the following constraints can be seen as restrictions on the paths.

1. The endpoint constraints $w(1) = 1$, $w(N) = M$, so that the respective endpoints of test and reference pattern are aligned.

2. Local variational constraints (Itakura, 1975)

$$0 \leq w(n) - w(n-1) \leq 2 \qquad (3.17a)$$

$$w(n) - w(n-1) = 0 \text{ iff } w(n-1) - w(n-2) > 0 \quad (3.17b)$$

Constraint (3.17a) ensures the path is monotonic and its slope is between 0 and 2. Constraint (3.17b) ensures the minimum average slope is $1/2$.

3. Global variational constraints, to define a parallelogram-shaped region which limits progressive local variations, so that the endpoint constraints are met. These constraints may be defined in terms of slope constraints for the alignment function (Levinson, 1985b) or in terms of a limitation upon m, $m_L(n) \leq m \leq m_H(n)$ (Brown and Rabiner, 1982) defined by

$$m_H(n) = \min\left\{2(n-1)+1, M - \tfrac{1}{2}(N-n), M\right\} \quad (3.18a)$$

$$m_L(n) = \max\left\{\tfrac{1}{2}(n-1)+1, M - 2(N-n), 1\right\} \quad (3.18b)$$

The search for alignments between test and reference pattern is a constrained dynamic programming problem (Bellman, 1959) in which the minimum accumulated distance between the patterns is given by the recursion

$$\begin{aligned}
D(n,m) = d(n,m) + \min\{ &D(n-1,m)g(n-1,m), \\
&D(n-1,m-1), \\
&D(n-1,m-2)\}
\end{aligned} \quad (3.19)$$

$$1 \leq n \leq N \quad \text{and} \quad m_L(n) \leq m \leq m_H(n)$$

$$\text{where } g(n,m) = 1 \text{ if } w(n) \neq w(n-1)$$
$$= \infty \quad \text{otherwise.}$$

The three recursive calls embody the local constraints (3.17), with the weighting function $g(n,m)$ used to enforce (3.17b) in the case where the alignment function advances on the test pattern, but not the reference pattern.

The minimum test-to-reference distance (3.16) is obtained from $D(N, M)$ by the recursion (3.19). It is possible but not essential to evaluate the alignment function $w(n)$; from the point of view of selecting a matching reference template, only the minimum distance between test and reference is required.

To recognize a vocabulary of speech patterns, a set of words for example, the template matching machine is trained by analysing given examples of the speech and storing the LP coefficients as templates. Recognition is then a decision as to which template best matches the input pattern, and this is achieved by selecting the template with the minimum test-to-reference pattern distance using the matching technique described above.

3.2.2. Hidden Markov models

Hidden Markov models (HMMs) have been used in ASR principally by Baker (1975), Jelinek (1976), and Levinson *et al* (1983). The technique is a parametric statistical method for the classification of observation sequences.

Speech patterns are again analysed as a sequence of short-time frames to produce a sequence of speech parameter-vectors such as LP coefficients. Each pattern, for example each word, is presented as a sequence of T observations in time, $\mathbf{O} = O_1, \ldots, O_t, \ldots, O_T$. The approach to recognition is again one of matching input patterns to stored reference patterns, but in this case each reference pattern is represented by a stochastic finite-state model.

The model has N states, $Q = \{q_1, \ldots, q_N\}$, and at any discrete time t the process is in some state q_i. The state may generate an *observation* at random, but each observation has a known probability of being generated from that state. The process then changes state to q_j at time $t + 1$ to generate the next observation. This next state is chosen at random, but each state transition has a known probability of occurring. An observer sees only the observations generated by a particular model, and not the "hidden" states and transitions.

Recognition is a decision as to which model best matches the given input pattern, and this is the model which has the highest probability of generating the given observation sequence. Suppose we wish to recognize a vocabulary of V words, $W = \{w_1, \ldots, w_V\}$. An utterance of some word $w_i \in W$ is presented as an observation sequence $\mathbf{O}$. Each word in the vocabulary is characterized by an HMM, with V HMMs, $\{M_1, \ldots, M_V\}$, for V words. The matching procedure is to calculate the combined probability, including both observation and transition probabilities, that the observation sequence $\mathbf{O}$ is generated by a particular model M_i. That is, the probability

$$P_i = \Pr(\mathbf{O}/M_i) \qquad (3.20)$$

for all $1 \leq i \leq V$ models.

The decision rule assigns observation sequence $\mathbf{O}$ to word w_i, as the word characterized by the model M_i which has the highest probability of generating the observation sequence $\mathbf{O}$:

$$w_i \text{ iff } P_i \geq P_j \text{ for all } j \neq i, \ 1 \leq j \leq V \qquad (3.21)$$

In the following paragraphs we will define HMMs and describe how to calculate the probability (3.20) of an observation sequence generated by a particular model. Finally we describe the estimation of model parameters, the observation and transition probabilities, from examples of known training patterns.

In the case of *discrete* HMMs, the observations are symbolic, usually derived from the codebook of a vector quantization process [5] (Buzo *et al.* 1980). In this case there is a discrete probability matrix which relates each symbol to each state,

$$\mathbf{B} = [b_{jk}]_{M \times N}, \quad b_{jk} = \Pr(v_k \text{ at } t \ / \ q_j \text{ at } t) \qquad (3.22)$$

where $v_k \in \{v_1, \ldots, v_M\}$, an alphabet of observed pattern primitives.

In the case of *continuous* HMMs, the matrix $\mathbf{B}$ is a vector of parameters for continuous probability density functions. These functions are usually Gaussian or a Gaussian mixture, and there is one function for each state. The observation sequence for continuous HMMs consists of vectors of speech parameters, and the density functions describe the probability that a particular vector is generated in a particular state. In the following discussion we shall consider discrete HMMs only.

It is assumed that the state sequences can be generated by a first-order Markov process; the extent of inter-state probabilistic dependence is limited to adjacent states. Therefore state transition is governed by a matrix

$$\mathbf{A} = [a_{ij}]_{N \times N}, \quad a_{ij} = \Pr(q_j \text{ at } t+1 \ / \ q_i \text{ at } t). \qquad (3.23)$$

The process can start in any state at random, but each state has a known probability of being the initial state. An initial state vector $\Pi = (\pi_1, \ldots, \pi_N)^t$ describes the discrete probability π_i that the model is in state q_i at time $t = 0$.

---

[5] In vector quantization, each vector of speech parameters, such as LP coefficients, is seen as a point in a multi-dimensional space. This space is *quantized* into regions, and each region is given a symbolic name from a *codebook* of names. A particular vector is assigned the symbol of the region within which it appears.

To summarize the model so far, the HMM is a doubly stochastic process with transition probabilities a_{ij} and observation probabilities b_{jk}. It is assumed that the observations are statistically independent events, that the transitions are dependent only upon adjacent states and are otherwise independent, and that the transitions are independent of the observations. The probability (3.20) can then be expressed as the joint probability of independent events, the observations and the state transitions.

For a particular model M_i, the probability for each state sequence of T observations is then

$$P = \pi_{q_1} b_{q_1}(O_1) \prod_{t=2}^{T} a_{q_{t-1}q_t} \cdot b_{q_t}(O_t) \qquad (3.24)$$

where $b_j(O_t) = b_{jk}$ when observation $O_t = v_k$, and the model is in state q_i at time $t-1$, state q_j at time t. Since there will be N^T mutually exclusive state sequences which generate T observations, the total probability for a particular observation sequence $\mathbf{O}$ given model M_i is

$$\Pr(\mathbf{O}/M_i) = \sum_{Q^T} \left(\pi_{q_1} b_{q_1}(O_1) \prod_{t=2}^{T} a_{q_{t-1}q_t} \cdot b_{q_t}(O_t) \right) \qquad (3.25)$$

where Q^T is the set of all N^T sequences of T states. Clearly it is not practical to evaluate (3.25) directly, and the usual approach is to factor out the search through the states of the model using either the forward-backward algorithm (Baum, 1972), or the Viterbi algorithm (Viterbi, 1967).

The forward-backward algorithm defines the forward probability $\alpha_t(i)$ as the total probability from the start to time t in state q_i, $\alpha_t(i) = \Pr(O_1 \ldots O_t/M)$. This can be formulated recursively in the following way:

$$\alpha_{t+1}(j) = \left[\sum_{i=1}^{N} \alpha_t(i) a_{ij} \right] b_j(O_{t+1}) \quad 1 \leq t \leq T-1 \quad (3.26)$$

with the stopping condition $\alpha_1(i) = \pi_i b_i(O_1)$. The backward probability $\beta_t(j)$ is defined as the total probability from time t in state q_j to the end at time T, $\beta_t(j) = \Pr(O_{t+1} \ldots O_T / M)$. This can also be formulated as a recursion:

$$\beta_t(i) = \sum_{j=1}^{N} a_{ij} b_j(O_{t+1}) \beta_{t+1}(j) \quad T-1 \geq t \geq 1 \quad (3.27)$$

with the stopping condition $\beta_T(j) = 1$. At any intermediate time t, the product of the forward and backward probabilities $\alpha_t(i) a_{ij} b_j(O_{t+1}) \beta_{t+1}(j)$ recursively computes the joint probability over all state sequences which include the transition from q_i to q_j. The total probability (3.25) is then calculated by summming over all state pairs:

$$\Pr(\mathbf{O}/M_i) = \sum_{i=1}^{N} \sum_{j=1}^{N} \alpha_t(i) a_{ij} b_j(O_{t+1}) \beta_{t+1}(j) \quad (3.28)$$

If we set $t = T - 1$ in (3.28) then there are no backward probabilities to calculate, and $\Pr(\mathbf{O}/M_i)$ can be computed from forward probabilities alone. Similarly, by setting $t = 1$ only the backward probabilities are required.

The Viterbi algorithm is a different formulation of (3.25). Instead of defining $\Pr(\mathbf{O}/M_i)$ as the joint sequence probability, define it as the maximum sequence probability, over all sequences. The solution is now a dynamic programming recursion:

$$\phi_t(j) = \max_{1 \le i \le N} \left[\phi_{t-1}(i)a_{ij}\right] b_j(O_t) \qquad (3.29)$$

for $2 \le t \le T$ and $1 \le j \le N$, with the stopping condition $\phi_1(i) = \pi_i b_i(O_1)$. Using this scheme the total probability is computed

$$\Pr(\mathbf{O}/M_i) = \max_{1 \le i \le N} \left[\phi_T(i)\right] \qquad (3.30)$$

The training procedure for HMMs is to estimate the parameters $\Pi, \mathbf{A}, \mathbf{B}$ from examples of known pattern data. For example, model M_i associated with word w_i is trained on utterences of w_i. The Baum-Welch algorithm (Baum, 1972) is a hill-climbing approach which aims to maximize the probability P (3.20) for model M_i over a set of training utterances of word w_i, by re-estimating the model parameters starting from some initial guesses.

The algorithm is specified by three re-estimation formulas which compute the probability, in terms of relative frequency, of the transitions, observations, and initial states respectively.

The transition probability a_{ij} is the relative frequency given by the expected number of transitions from state q_i to q_j, divided by the expected number of all transitions out of q_i. These expected numbers can be expressed in terms of the forward and backward probabilities, as follows. The expected number of transitions from q_i to q_j is

$$\gamma_{ij} = \frac{1}{P} \sum_{t=1}^{T-1} \alpha_t(i)a_{ij}b_j(O_{t+1})\beta_{t+1}(j) \qquad (3.31)$$

This is simply the frequency of all state sequences which include the transition q_i to q_j, relative to the frequency of all sequences (3.28). The expected number of transitions out of q_i is, using (3.27),

$$\gamma_i = \sum_{j=1}^{N} \gamma_{ij} = \frac{1}{P} \sum_{t=1}^{T-1} \alpha_t(i)\beta_t(i) \qquad (3.32)$$

Given γ_{ij} and γ_i from a previous estimate or an initial guess, the re-estimated transition probability is the relative frequency given by the ratio γ_{ij}/γ_i,

$$\hat{a}_{ij} = \frac{\sum_{t=1}^{T-1} \alpha_t(i)a_{ij}b_j(O_{t+1})\beta_{t+1}(j)}{\sum_{t=1}^{T-1} \alpha_t(i)\beta_t(i)} \qquad (3.33)$$

In a similar way the observation probability b_{jk} is the frequency of the occurrence of symbol v_k in state q_j relative to the occurrence of any symbol in state q_j. The new estimate for b_{jk} can be expressed in terms of the forward and backward probabilities,

$$\hat{b}_{jk} = \frac{\sum_{T^k} \alpha_t(j)\beta_t(j)}{\sum_{t=1}^{T} \alpha_t(j)\beta_t(j)} \qquad (3.34)$$

where T^k denotes the set of all t, $1 \leq t \leq T$, for which $O_t = v_k$.

The initial state probability π_i is the frequency of the occurrence of q_i as the initial state relative to the occurrence of any initial state. The new estimate for π_i is then

$$\hat{\pi}_i = \frac{1}{P}\alpha_1(i)\beta_1(i) \qquad (3.35)$$

The re-estimation formulas (3.33)(3.34)(3.35) are guaranteed to incrementally increase P (Levinson *et al.* 1983), but this hill-climbing approach does not guarantee to be climbing the highest possible hill. The training procedure is not optimal because P can only be locally maximized.

Clearly the assymptotic value for P depends upon the choice of initial estimates, and in practice a range of initial guesses should be tried. Also on a practical note, some scaling procedure should be used to prevent arithmetic underflow, since $\alpha \to 0$ and $\beta \to 0$ as $T \to \infty$. The parameter estimates are assymptotically unbiased as $T \to \infty$, but this requires a lot of observations. It is also possible for the re-estimation process to become trapped in a situation when $b_{jk} = 0$ for some training sequence. Solutions to these practical problems are described by Levinson *et al* (1983).

3.2.3. Trade-offs between template matching and hidden Markov models

Both the speech pattern recognition methods described above have demonstrated excellent results for the restricted tasks of isolated digit or word recognition (Rabiner and Levinson, 1981; Rabiner *et al*. 1983). In particular the HMM approach provides a degree of speaker independence not shown by the template matching methods. A detailed comparison of these methods is given by Juang (1984). A few general conclusions can be drawn as follows.

Templates are easy to train, but costly to use. HMMs are costly to train but easy to use (Rabiner *et al*. 1983). The training procedure for templates is the time taken to extract a sufficient range of prototypes, and this can be done in a matter of a few minutes. The training procedure for HMMs requires a massive amount of training data, and can run for days to weeks depending on the complexity of the model. The matching procedure for templates is more computationally intensive than that for HMMs, so that once the models are trained the HMM is generally faster in recognition than the template matching machine.

Templates have no provision for modelling local structural variations, and consequently the templates are particularly speaker dependent. It is usually necessary to record a number of templates for each of a number of possible renderings of a particular word. HMMs model local structural variations by providing a weighting for alternative sequences of states and observations, and as a result are somewhat less speaker dependent than templates. For both types of model such variations must be sufficiently distributed across the training data. Performance is degraded unless such variation is represented, especially in word-medial position (Rabiner *et al.* 1982).

Although the methods of template matching by dynamic time alignment and HMMs are formulated in quite different ways, they are actually quite closely related in principle. Both are techniques for sequential pattern classification, with the template method using a matching criterion based upon distance, and the HMM using a probabilistic criterion. The close relationship between methods of pattern classification based upon distance and upon probability is discussed in Chapter 5. The algorithms which enumerate pattern sequences all rely upon a Markovian relationship between successive elements in sequence. In the case of the dynamic programming algorithm for template matching, the alignment path constraints effect the first-order Markov property, while for HMMs this property is implicit in the use of state-transition matrices. The procedure of template matching by dynamic time alignment can be seen as a special or constrained case of HMM (Bridle, 1984).

3.2.4. The problem of local optimality

Although the methods described above can give excellent results when applied to a restricted task such as isolated digit or word recognition, some serious difficulties arise when they are applied to more ambitious tasks such as connected word recognition. The source of the difficulties with more complex problems is the source of the advantages with simpler problems, and that is that the models are simple enough so that parameter estimation is tractable.

There are inherent limitations due to the underlying assumptions made by the model. In the case of templates the assumptions are based upon the nature of the metric and upon the dynamic programming path constraints, in the case of HMMs upon the form of the probability distributions and the Markovian assumption. Though each may be optimal in its own way, there is no guarantee that the model used is the best for characterization of all kinds of speech pattern. In the case of discrete HMMs, it can be argued that the probabilities in the B-matrix are optimal over all possible distribution functions. However this is merely shifting the responsibility down to the vector quantizer, which has to characterize the continuous distributions of multi-dimensional random variables in terms of a discrete alphabet or *codebook*.

An important disadvantage of these methods is that neither has an inherent mechanism for weighting the most informative parts of a pattern. Certain small-scale details of a pattern are crucially important for the discrimination of confusible sets of words. For example the essential differences between `rapid` and `rabbit` (the initial syllable vowel duration, the closure duration, and possibly the aspiration of /p/) are de-emphasized, and this important detail is swamped by the general similarity of the confusible patterns. This is an example of the models limitation due to its *local* optimality. Although the model may be optimal, in the maximum likelihood sense, for each word in the vocabulary, there is no provision for a more *global* optimality which would take into consideration the optimal discrimination of different words.

The formulation of the model leads to a local optimality which is a great advantage when the important sources of constraint and discrimination are also local. However when these sources of constraint and discrimination are distributed over a variety of levels and scales, then local optimality criteria are no longer sufficient. From the viewpoint of language acquisition, the machine which discovers certain categories in the data must have some justification for the selection of one set of categories, one set of selected features and so forth, in preference to another. This requires a global knowledge of pattern discrimination which extends from the most primitive representation of the patterns right up to the ideas and meanings attached to the patterns, and this knowledge is not available to a locally optimal process. So although it is possible to identify categories which are locally distinct, it is not possible to claim the machine discovered categories of global significance, without the use of tacit knowledge to guide the feature selection appropriately, and to identify global significance when it appears.

Perhaps the main drawback with the pattern matching methods described, and indeed with any method based on whole-word pattern matching, is simply that the word is not a practical recognition unit for unrestricted speech recognition. There are just too many words to store models of.

3.3. Models with hierarchical structure

The use of whole-word models, as described in the previous section, is impractical for a large vocabulary. However, many words share segments of speech (the English language is approximately 50% redundant in the information-theoretic sense), so that the number of essential pattern-matching models can be greatly reduced. The choice of a set of speech segments, or *recognition units*, to unambiguously represent all words depends upon three factors, described in the following sections. These are the number of units, their numerical invariance, and the generality of the hierarchical structure through which sequences of such units are systematically combined into words.

3.3.1. Why is hierarchical structure important?

> " No human language has a limit on the number of sentences which are properly formed and that receive a semantic interpretation in accordance with the rules of this language. However the grammar of each language must obviously be a finite object, realized physically in a finite human brain. Therefore one component of the grammar must have a recursive property ... which is the syntactic component." (Chomsky and Halle, 1968 p.6)

The implication which follows from this is that there are

some principles, contained in a language acquisition component of the brain, which operate to guide the formation of grammars for the structural representation of information. It is not unreasonable to suppose that the principles used to guide the formation of language also guide the formation of speech. In this case the syntactic component extends below patterns of words through a hierarchy of category domains, to derive patterns of elementary acoustic features. Every aspect of the speech signal which originates in a controlled articulatory intention is part of the structured formation of speech.

Of course any information-bearing signal can be seen from a recognition viewpoint in purely quantitative terms, as pattern vectors. The idea of imposing a structure on a pattern follows from the fact that it is intrinsically easier to describe a complex pattern in terms of smaller, less complex, pattern components. That this notion is intuitively true may well be a reflection of the nature of human cognitive processes; in any case structure is, and has been at least since the turn of the century, an essential part of our understanding of speech and language.

On computational grounds, the exploitation of a structural hierarchy over a language of patterns is a method for summarising the description of pattern variations, which has complexity advantages in both the representation and application of pattern knowledge. Generality in a grammar is the ability to represent the pattern language with the most economical set of rules. This implies that grammatical constituents have been chosen to capture particularly significant generalizations of structural regularities.

Generality reduces complexity through the idea of sharing. The idea is that nodes in the parse tree are shared by different derivations, so that unnecessary duplication is avoided. For example, an infinite number of sentences in the English language can be represented by a finite number of words, with an appropriate grammar to generate the sentences, because sentences share words. There are upward of 100,000 words in the English language, but these can be represented by some 4000 syllables, with an appropriate grammar to generate words from syllables. These syllables may in turn be represented by about 40 phonemes, again through an appropriate grammar. In general, the exploitation of structure, through the idea of sharing, reduces the size of the set of terminal symbols, and this is a great advantage when these symbols represent the basic recognition units used in pattern matching.

It would seem impractical, for both human and machine, to store reference patterns of whole words if the size of the vocabulary is to be unrestricted. Perhaps the syllable is a reasonable choice for recognition unit, but it turns out that the number of syllables, when all prosodic and allophonic variants are included, is something over 30,000. However the set of phonemes, including all their allophonic variants, is only about 150. On consideration of the number of units, the phoneme, or perhaps the diphone, is then a practical recognition unit. Two important questions follow which concern the numerical invariance of phoneme-sized units (from the viewpoint of pattern matching), and the inference of hierarchical structure (syllable and word grammars) over the set of phoneme sequences.

3.3.2. Numerical invariance and context dependency

By numerical invariance we mean the tendency of feature vectors, derived from measurements of a particular category of speech segment, to cluster in a characteristic region of the feature space. The key property of such clusters is that the feature space may be partitioned, for example using one of the methods described in Chapter 5, so as to discriminate between the various different categories of speech segment. The discriminating power of a pattern classifier can be measured by a performance index, such as the ratio of inter-class distance to intra-class variance described in Chapter 5. We wish to choose categories of speech segment for which a selected set of descriptive features is relatively invariant, so as to maximize a performance index in terms of the power to discriminate between the speech categories.

The perceptual invariance of a speech category refers to the invariance of the percept with respect to some subjective assessment of the intra-category similarity or the inter-category contrast of speech sounds. Ideally we wish to select a set of features to describe a speech segment such that the numerical invariance corresponds with the perceptual invariance. This goal can be approached through a judicious feature selection (see Chapter 4), but in general there is a discrepancy between the percieved equivalence classes and their corresponding numerical representations, which appear to have a lot more intra-class variance. This variation, which is due to speaker and linguistic context, should cause pattern classes to overlap, with a resulting loss in discriminating power. That there are perceptually invariant classes suggests that there is some normalization process at work during perceptual classification which accounts for class variations due to speaker and linguistic context.

We might suppose that speaker dependent variations and those dependent upon linguistic context be considered as two distinct problems, so that the former problem can be delegated to a global speaker-adaptation process. This is discussed briefly in Chapter 6, but we will consider normalization processes dependent only upon linguistic context.

There are probably two components of this normalization process: an inherent or context-free component, and a context-dependent component. The inherent normalization of the speech signal (of which a simple example might be an automatic gain control) is a function of the signal analysis which takes place in the peripheral auditory system. The context dependent normalization requires a certain amount of memory. It is then important to consider what the basic unit of speech perception is, and over what scale the context dependency operates.

From a consideration of the number of units required, units of at most phoneme-size appear to be the practical choice. But there are coarticulatory effects between phonemes that span the duration of a syllable. Reaction time experiments (Kozhevnikov and Chistovich, 1978) show that although the basic unit of speech recognition may be the phoneme, the segment of speech required to define a phoneme is at least a consonant-vowel segment, or a consonant-vowel syllable. Reaction times in speech perception indicate that the normalization process for phonetic classification is complete at the syllabic level, and takes place over a consonant-vowel. We note that the effects of classification based upon un-normalized data are "averaged out" over the rather artificial situation of a whole-word model. Thus it is possible to obtain a reasonable degree of word discrimination using the methods of whole-word pattern matching when the size and general confusibility of the vocabulary is restricted.

One particular type of reaction test is distinguished by remarkably fast reaction times, and this is the speech shadowing experiment (Kozhevnikov and Chistovich, 1978; Marslen-Wilson and Tyler, 1981) which measures speech reaction times to speech stimuli. It has been suggested (Porter and Lubker, 1980) that the very early stages of speech perceptual analysis yield information which is converted directly into the information required for speech production, and that this special ability enables shadowing responses which are "almost as fast as responses of their type can possibly be". We could also account for the success of speech shadowing by supposing that both processes share knowledge of phonotactic and allophonic variation, implicit in some representation of well-formed phoneme sequences. Phonemes are classified in sequences which evolve in time under constraints, dependent upon the articulator positions, which are both physiological and linguistic. The precise (normalized) definition of phonemes may not be available to higher processing levels until a syllable has evolved, but sufficient low-level information is available to the speech production process.

The shadowing experiments support the motor theory of speech perception (Galunov and Chistovich, 1966; Wathen-Dunn, 1967) which explicitly links the perception and production processes. It is concluded that some categorization arises at the earliest stage of the perceptual process. These categories and their associated linguistic constraints, which are common to both perception and production processes, make it possible to successfully shadow speech before it is actually percieved. In effect, at the syllabic level we percieve what *is* said in the light of a time-evolving knowledge of what *could* be said.

This suggests that the context-dependent normalization process required for optimal phonetic classification is based upon a model of well-formed sequences of articulation categories, generalized at the level of the syllable. We hypothesize that the apparent normalization which takes place is actually a result of the categorization and feature selection of speech sounds, correlated with the motoric information required by the speech production process. If this is true we can expect a model of allophonic and phonotactic effects to account for the numerical variations due to linguistic context. This structural model describes the context in terms of primitive articulation categories, and within a given context we can expect a specialized category to have less-variant numerical characteristics.

3.3.3. The inference problem

In the general case, a hierarchical structure is derived from a grammar which has a generative power at least equivalent to context-free grammar. However the automatic inference of context-free grammar from training observations cannot be accomplished because the problem of establishing the equivalence of context-free grammars is undecidable (Aho and Ullman, 1972 p199).

The linguistic parallel to the computational process of grammatical inference is called the *descriptive method* (Harris, 1951), and is motivated purely by observations of behaviour. The method involves a catalogue to be made of all the kinds of structures found in a corpus of naturally occurring pattern data. This catalogue is a list of the prominent regularities and their taxonomic inter-relationships which occur in the data, compiled under strict experimental conditions according to prescribed criteria.

A serious problem with the descriptive method is that it lacks the capability for making intuitive decisions which lead to a more adequate structure. The *adequacy* of a generative grammar is a justification for its selection over another grammar. From a linguistic (Chomsky, 1957) point of view, the term adequacy describes how well a grammar reflects the speakers tacit knowledge of language or *linguistic competence*. Humans are capable of forming structural theories, but the principles by which one structural theory is selected over others are unknown. The principles of such a meta-theory of language acquisition are not observable, and neither can they be extracted from data by any known inductive process. In addition, these principles operate to form structural theories over the entire world model on which human cognitive processes are based, and therefore an entirely adequate structure cannot be inferred from observations of speech data alone.

In order to improve the descriptive method for classification of a language it is necessary to make the blind search for pattern regularity somewhat more creatively. This is the approach of *generative linguistics* (Chomsky, 1957). Rather than follow rigorous procedures for analyzing a language by observation, the generative linguist makes use of intuitions based on his or her native language abilities. The approach is to tap into the world model in order to gain some intuitions for the construction of principled theories. In this sense the formulation of structural theories based on speech knowledge need not be seen as an essentially *ad hoc* process. These structural theories are expressed as formal grammar rules, and provided the theory is consistent, and consistently adhered to, there should be no excuse for rules which compete with or contradict each other.

3.4. Phonetic knowledge in automatic speech recognition

It is not possible to automatically infer an optimal hierarchical structure over the set of sequences of recognition units. Therefore it is essential to motivate structure top-down, employing a knowledge of the inherent constraints in speech and language. The use of principled linguistic theory can approach an optimality in the sense of structural generality, and also in the sense of numerical invariance, when the structure accounts for the context dependency of normalization processes for perceptually invariant categories. If we choose a phoneme-sized recognition unit, then we must consider the pattern-matching process, and the structure of phonetic sequences. The pattern-matching process, feature extraction and classification, is described in Chapters 4 and 5. The structure of phoneme sequences is based upon a phonetic knowledge of syllable structure, which is introduced in the following sections, and expanded in Chapter 6.

3.4.1. Kinds of phonetic knowledge

Acoustic-phonetic knowledge concerns the nature of the feature complexes which cue particular phonetic categories in particular contexts. It is well known that acoustic correlates combine in varying degrees to cue a phonetic category. The study of acoustic correlates and their integration to form cues is an important and incomplete area of acoustic-phonetics. The reader is referred to Jakobson, Fant and Halle (1952), Fant (1973), and Ladefoged (1982).

Phonetic categories are based upon singular events in the manner and place of articulation of a speech sound. The manner of articulation refers to the type of obstruction made by the tongue and lips, and the degree of voicing, during production of a speech sound. Categories distinguished by their manner of articulation include the vowels, voiced and unvoiced stops and fricatives, liquids, nasals, glides, and affricates. These categories are sub-divided into phonemes according to the place of articulation, which refers to the position of the main obstruction. For example the manner of articulation class "voiced stop" contains the phonemes /b/ /d/ /g/ each distinguished by the place of articulation, which is at the lips, the alveolar ridge, and the velum or soft palate respectively.

The phoneme functions as an abstract linguistic unit for describing speech sounds. The inventory of phonemes is based upon the set of smallest contrastive units, but the contrast is measured in terms of human perception abilities. In these terms it is possible to consider speech as a sequence of discrete phonetic segments, in spite of the fact that the continuous nature of articulatory processes in speech production means that the acoustic correlates of a given phoneme can change considerably depending upon the immediate phonetic context. This contextual dependency is called coarticulation, with reference to the fact that the precise position of the articulators for a given phoneme is influenced by the preceding phoneme, and the anticipation of the following phoneme.

The nature of the context dependency between phonetic categories is another important part of acoustic-phonetic knowledge. Coarticulatory variation can be formulated to an extent by allophonic rules. These are context-sensitive re-write rules which describe the allophonic variants of a phoneme in different contexts. An allophone is a particular phonetic realization of a phoneme according to its context. For example the word `little` has two allophones of the phoneme /l/, the so-called "light" and "dark" /l/ respectively.

In general, even an allophone of a given phoneme will, in different utterances, show considerable phonetic differences.

The allophone is certainly not an invariant speech category, it is however less variant, and furthermore its relationship to abstract linguistic units is defined by rule. It is therefore an information-bearing category worthy of some attention, and should not be discarded simply because it fails to be uniformly invariant, in terms of its acoustic correlates, across a range of speakers.

There is evidence that knowledge of allophonic variations is helpful in phonetic decoding, and that such variations are in fact sources of information rather than contributors of noise (Kahn, 1968; Church, 1983). Recognition based upon sound categories is an attractive paradigm provided the variations in the complex of acoustic correlates are systematic and can be finitely represented. Support for this hypothesis is provided by the spectrogram reading experiments of Cole and Zue (1980), which show the adequacy of local spectral information for phonetic decoding. It is also helpful to know that there are considerable constraints upon sequences of linguistic units. Tables of English phonotactic possibilities (Gimson, 1984) show that by no means all of the possible combinations of phonemes are actually used.

Clearly there exists speech knowledge which can be exploited to improve the performance of phonetic decoding of continuous speech. However this is a long-term research goal. Basic research into knowledge representation and reasoning is required for the appropriate application of the wealth of acoustic-phonetic knowledge which has accumulated over the years.

At one time it was believed that primitive feature extraction was not as crucial to overall performance as it is believed to be today. During the famous ARPA speech project of the early 1970's much emphasis was placed upon the higher level structural constraints of word syntax and semantics, in the hope that such constraints would be sufficient to disambiguate the large number of candidates produced by the so called "quick and dirty" front end processes. One of the great lessons of ARPA is that higher level constraints are generally not sufficient for this task. It is interesting to note that in the more recent major push towards automatic speech recognition in America, the DARPA projects (Sears, 1985), there appears to be relatively little energy, in terms of expert representation on the projects, devoted to higher level constraints, and the emphasis is once more on basic research into lower level acoustic-phonetics.

3.4.2. Context-free grammar as a vehicle for phonetic knowledge

Gazdar (1982) claims that patterns of words in natural language can be adequately described by context-free grammar. This claim is naturally very difficult to prove, but recent work (Joshi and Levy, 1982) seems to indicate a growing consensus in its favour. It is therefore plausible that patterns in sub-syllabic categories, where structural theories can account for phonological and allophonic variations, may also be adequately described by context-free grammar. But is it necessary to use context-free grammar at this level?

The main advantage of context-free grammar is that it provides a method, inherent within the pattern representation, for focusing the attention of the recognizer upon the most informative parts of the pattern. As has been said, it is necessary to focus upon particular informative parts of the pattern, in order to improve fine phonetic distinctions. A context-free grammar representation can isolate particular pattern components which show important and distinct variants. This is achieved by re-formulating context-sensitive re-write rules as context-free rules so as to capture significant linguistic generalizations. In an example given by Church (1983), the allophonic rule which expresses the aspiration of /t/ (denoted t^h) in pre-vocalic position

$$t \rightarrow t^h / \#\_V$$

can be re-formulated as part of a context-free grammar of

syllable structure:

$$\text{syllable} \rightarrow \text{onset, rhyme.}$$
$$\text{onset} \rightarrow t^h \mid k^h \mid p^h \ldots$$
$$\text{rhyme} \rightarrow \text{peak, coda.}$$
$$\text{coda} \rightarrow t^g \mid k^g \mid p^g \ldots$$

where $/t^g/$ indicates an unreleased or glottalized $/t/$.

In this way the context or environment common to a group of allophonic variants can be isolated, and their underlying characterizations can be specialized. In addition the generality of categories leads to an economy of representation, where a category is defined in a single context-free rule instead of in every allophonic rule.

A context-free grammar such as the above syllable grammar, which has no recursive productions, can be translated directly into a finite state network. Such a grammar therefore has much in common with other network-oriented systems such as HARPY (Lowerre, 1976). When quantitative information is incorporated, as illustrated in Chapter 2, then the common recognition procedure is finding the highest scoring path through a network. The advantage of context-free rules is that they are comprehensible; it is important for an evolving knowledge-based system to remain comprehensible to the human expert. Significant generalities of structure and specialized points of contrast are made explicit in the grammatical representation. If the expression of a linguistic theory requires a degree of context dependence, then this can be incorporated by augmenting the context-free grammer, for example as described in Chapter 2. The provision of such constraints in the form of alternative network pathways compounds the complexity of network representations.

3.5. Summary

We have described the two principal techniques of whole-word pattern matching used in modern speech recognition. The template matching method and the hidden Markov model illustrate the advantages of a well-formulated pattern matching machine which uses optimality criteria based upon maximum likelihood. However there are general limitations to the use of whole-word models in unrestricted speech recognition. Whole-word models tend to "average out" discriminatory detail which exists at the phonetic level. This can be an advantage when the recognition unit contains a lot of redundant information, as is the case for whole-words selected from a relatively small vocabulary, but as the size of the vocabulary grows, so the power to discriminate between words decreases.

We have discussed how to represent a language economically by sharing linguistic constituents in a hierarchy, and we pointed out that due to the inference problem this hierarchical structure must be motivated by *a priori* linguistic knowledge. We have argued that the application of principled linguistic theory leads to a kind of optimality in the sense of economy of representation, by capturing significant generalities of structure, and also in classification performance, by isolating less-variant categories of special importance for pattern discrimination.

By considering the psycho-linguistic evidence we conclude that categorization of speech sounds arises at a low level. Perceptual invariance results from a context-dependent normalization process operating at or below the level of the syllable. This normalization process may be inherent in a categorization of speech sounds, and a model of category sequences, which is directly related to the speech production process. A promising line of approach is suggested, in which linguistic knowledge in the form of allophonic rules and phonotactic constraints can be incorporated into an augmented context-free grammar based upon syllable structure.

CHAPTER 4
Feature extraction

4.1. Introduction

The classification of patterns as performed by humans is based upon the satisfaction of numerous constraints on the sensory attributes of the pattern. For pattern classification by sequential machine, where computational economy is of importance, the approach is to select the minimum number of attributes or *significant features* of the pattern which are required for classification. The amount of computation required for classification, and the amount of data required for training, grows exponentially with the dimensionality of the feature space. This inevitable result is what Bellman (1957) called "the curse of dimensionality". The justification for a selection of features is the reduction of data, so that a computationally feasible classification algorithm is applicable, concomitant with classifier performance. This implies that there are well known types of algorithm for pattern classification, and that their performance is directly measureable, in terms of error rates or inter-class distances, reflecting the discriminating power of the classifier. Types of pattern classification algorithm and associated performance measures are discussed in Chapter 5.

Feature extraction is basically a transformation of the measurement data into pattern data, such that the space of the pattern data has a lower dimensionality than that of the measurement data. An n-vector of measurements is transformed into an m-vector, $m < n$, of features in the pattern or feature space. An important property of such a transformation is that it is *information preserving*, that is, that the data is reduced by removing redundant components, but preserving in some optimal sense that information which is crucial to pattern discrimination. The efficacy of a particular feature extraction process in preserving the requisite information can be seen in the performance of the subsequent classifiers.

If significant features are known *a priori*, then feature extraction amounts to the implementation of specific *property detectors*. However the optimal significant features are generally not known and must be sought in the data.

A very simple *feature selection* procedure is to remove one measurement at a time, maintaining the highest value in some performance index in terms of the remaining measurements. Variables are removed until there is an unacceptable degradation in the pattern information. In Chapter 5 we discuss several metric and probabilistic measures of classifier performance in terms of pattern-class separation in the feature space, and these measures can be used to guide the feature selection from the viewpoint of discrimination between multiple classes. In the following section we consider feature selection from the viewpoint of information preservation in individual pattern classes.

In general the simple approach of feature removal is not adequate, and it is necessary to find some transformation which projects the measurements onto a lower subspace, motivated by some criterion of optimality. If we restrict this transformation to a linear combination of measurements, then it is possible to find the optimal transformation in a least mean-squared error sense using a technique of feature selection based upon the Karhunen-Loéve (K-L) expansion of the measurement data.

4.2. The Karhunen-Loéve expansion in feature selection

The K-L expansion is a technique based upon matrix factorization for explaining the covariance structure of a signal, which can be used in a feature selection procedure to arrive at a more parsimonious description of the signal. Let a real signal $x(t)$ be represented as a point in a vector space, where the coordinate axes are a set of mutually orthogonal *basis functions*. The signal is therefore defined by its position in this space, and this is represented by a set of coefficients, one for each basis function. The *orthogonal expansion* of a signal is a norm of the signal vector, defined:

$$x(t) = \sum_{i=1}^{\infty} c_i \phi_i(t) \tag{4.1}$$

where the c_i are random uncorrelated coefficients, and the $\phi_i(t)$ are the orthogonal basis functions, normalized such that

$$E\big[\phi_i(t)\phi_j(t)\big] = \begin{cases} 1 & i = j \\ 0 & i \neq j \end{cases}$$

where $E[\cdot]$ denotes the expected value.

The Fourier series is a special case of (4.1) which uses sinusoidal basis functions. Although a non-periodic process cannot be expanded as a Fourier series with uncorrelated coefficients, such a process can in general be expanded as a series of orthogonal functions $\phi_i(t)$.

In practice, a signal $x(t)$ is represented as a point in a finite space of n-dimensions by sampling the signal in some interval. The signal is then a *signal vector* $x = (x_1, \ldots, x_n)^t$. The orthogonal basis functions $\phi_i(t)$ are similarly sampled, so that the ith coordinate axis is a *base vector* $q_i = (\phi_{i1}, \ldots, \phi_{in})^t$, and these vectors are arranged as the columns of an orthogonal matrix $\mathbf{Q} = \left(q_1, \ldots, q_n\right)$, normalized such that $\mathbf{Q}^t\mathbf{Q} = \mathbf{I}$, the unit matrix. With the coefficients represented by $c = \left(c_1, \ldots, c_n\right)^t$, we can re-write (4.1) as the finite sum

$$x = \mathbf{Q}c \tag{4.2}$$

This is known as the Karhunen-Loéve expansion of the signal $x(t)$. The expansion is characterized by the coefficients c, and it is possible to calculate these coefficients from (4.2) by re-arranging to give

$$c = \mathbf{Q}^t x \tag{4.3}$$

This is possible if $\mathbf{Q}$ is an orthonormal matrix, having the important property $\mathbf{Q}^t\mathbf{Q} = \mathbf{I}$. We can now calculate the coefficients of the expansion because, as we will see, $\mathbf{Q}$ is the matrix of normalized column eigenvectors of the signal covariance matrix.

We will use the covariance matrix as the basic description of the signal, and assuming a zero mean signal for the K-L expansion we define it as

$$\mathbf{R} = \mathrm{E}\left[xx^t\right] \tag{4.4}$$

A necessary assumption for the K-L expansion is that the signal has zero mean. Under this assumption we can derive a relationship between the matrix $\mathbf{R}$ and the orthogonal matrix of base vectors $\mathbf{Q}$ as follows. Substituting (4.2) for x into (4.4) we have

$$\begin{aligned}
\mathbf{R} &= \mathrm{E}\left[\mathbf{Q}c(\mathbf{Q}c)^t\right] \\
&= \mathrm{E}\left[\mathbf{Q}cc^t\mathbf{Q}^t\right] \\
&= \mathbf{Q}\mathrm{E}\left[cc^t\right]\mathbf{Q}^t
\end{aligned}$$

The last step is valid since $\mathbf{Q}$ is deterministic. Because c is uncorrelated, the matrix cc^t is diagonal, and so let the expected value be

$$E\left[cc^t\right] = \Lambda = \begin{pmatrix} \lambda_1 & & \bigcirc \\ & \ddots & \\ \bigcirc & & \lambda_n \end{pmatrix}$$

so that

$$\mathbf{R} = \mathbf{Q}\Lambda\mathbf{Q}^t \tag{4.5}$$

The quadratic form in (4.5) can be identified as the *spectral decomposition* of the symmetric matrix $\mathbf{R}$. This will be discussed in relation to clustering transformations on the feature space in Chapter 5, but suffice it to say that any real symmetric matrix can be factored in the form (4.5), where Λ is the diagonal matrix of eigenvalues, and $\mathbf{Q}$ is the matrix of corresponding normalized column eigenvectors, which are mutually orthogonal. So we see that the ith base vector used in the expansion (4.2) is just the ith eigenvector of the covariance matrix $\mathbf{R}$. We can compute the eigenvectors using one of the well known algorithms[1] and use (4.3) to find the coefficients of the expansion.

The K-L expansion of a signal (4.1) can be generalized to vector valued signals if we interpret each stretch of n samples in the expected value (4.4) as one multivariate data vector $x = (x_1, \ldots, x_n)^t$. If $k > n$ vectors are arranged in an $n \times k$ data matrix $\mathbf{X} = (x^{(1)}, \ldots, x^{(k)})$ then

$$\mathbf{X}\mathbf{X}^t = E\left[xx^t\right] \tag{4.6}$$

---

[1] See Wilkinson and Reinsch (1971) or Golub and Van Loan (1983) for theory and description, and see Businger (1965) for a program listing to compute the eigenvalues and eigenvectors of a real symmetric matrix.

and from (4.5), the spectral decomposition of the matrix $\mathbf{X}\mathbf{X}^t$

$$\begin{aligned}\mathbf{\Lambda} &= \mathbf{Q}^t(\mathbf{X}\mathbf{X}^t)\mathbf{Q} \\ &= \mathbf{Q}^t\mathbf{X}(\mathbf{Q}^t\mathbf{X})^t \\ &= \mathbf{Z}\mathbf{Z}^t\end{aligned} \tag{4.7}$$

where $\mathbf{Z} = (c^{(1)}, \ldots, c^{(k)})$ is the matrix of expansion co-efficients. If the signal is stationary over k stretches of n samples, or over k samples of n-vectors (whichever way you look at it), then the signal statistics remain constant, and so each stretch or vector has the same orthogonal set of principal axes, but each has a particular vector of coefficients. We can compute the matrix $\mathbf{Q}$ (the eigenvectors of $\mathbf{X}\mathbf{X}^t$), and using the orthogonal transformation, from (4.7) (corresponding to (4.3)),

$$\mathbf{Z} = \mathbf{Q}^t\mathbf{X} \tag{4.8}$$

find the coefficients in the expansion for each data vector.

The coefficients vector c of the K-L expansion is a trans-formed representation of the signal vector x which makes explicit the relative significance of each of a set of mutually orthogonal base vectors describing the signal. These coeffi-cients represent the new variables in the transformed space. The covariance matrix of the coefficients $\mathrm{E}\left[cc^t\right] = \mathbf{Z}\mathbf{Z}^t$, and from (4.7) it is clear that this is diagonal so that these vari-ables are uncorrelated. The transformation (4.3) and (4.8) (see also section 5.2.2) is a rigid rotation which aligns the principal axes (the orthogonal set with extremal values of variance) of the covariance matrix with the coordinate axes of the feature space. The transformed variables in each vector c are independent orthogonal components of the signal which are ordered, corresponding with the eigenvalues, according to their contribution of variance to the signal. We note also that the rows of matrix Z are a set of n time functions, $c_i^{(1)}, \ldots, c_i^{(k)}$, $1 \leq i \leq n$, each the result of a transformation $q_i^t X$, so that the time function which corresponds to the largest eigenvalue contains most of the characteristics of the original signal, and that which corresponds to the smallest eigenvalue contains only residual low-variance characteristics of the signal.

Feature selection based on the K-L expansion of a signal obtains a low-dimensional representation of the signal by discarding the residual low-variance components. We effectively discard those terms in the expansion (4.2) which contribute least to the sum, and retain those terms which account for most of the variance. The selection of $m < n$ features (variables) is then the appropriate transformation using the m eigenvectors q_i which correspond to the m largest eigenvalues λ_i. If we re-define Q as an $n \times m$ matrix to retain the m column eigenvectors corresponding to the m largest eigenvalues of XX^t, then following (4.3) the coefficient vector c is now an m-vector, and we take this as the representation of signal vector x with lower dimensionality. Similarly, following (4.8) the coefficient matrix Z consists of k m-vectors, and we take this as the representation of the data matrix X with lower dimensionality.

Selecting a representation of $m < n$ dimensions is an approximation which is bound to cause some error, $e = x - Qc$. The particular advantage of the K-L expansion in feature selection is that it can be shown (Kendall, 1975 pp16–17) that the error due to selecting $m < n$ features is minimized in the least mean-squared sense. In this sense there is no better linear method for selecting features. There is another optimal property associated with the K-L expansion, which is the clustering property of the image vectors c in the transformed space, and this is discussed in Chapter 5.

The method of finding the eigenvectors Q by the spectral decomposition of XX^t is, however, prone to inaccuracy due to rounding errors introduced during the computation of

$\mathbf{X}\mathbf{X}^t$ (Stewart, 1973 p382). What is required is to obtain $\mathbf{Q}$ by a direct decomposition of the data matrix $\mathbf{X}$. A matrix $\mathbf{X}_{[n \times k]}$, with $n < k$, cannot in general be diagonalized, but a factorization which approximates this is the *singular value decomposition* (SVD) (Eckart and Young, 1939),

$$\mathbf{X} = \mathbf{Q}\Delta\mathbf{P}^t \qquad (4.9)$$

where $\mathbf{Q}_{[n \times n]}$ and $\mathbf{P}_{[k \times k]}$ are orthonormal (unitary) matrices, and $\Delta_{[n \times k]}$ contains the singular values $\sigma_1, \ldots, \sigma_n$ on the principal diagonal, and is zero elsewhere. The singular values are uniquely determined, and are related to the eigenvalues Λ of $\mathbf{X}\mathbf{X}^t$ in that $\Delta = \Lambda^{\frac{1}{2}}$. The columns of $\mathbf{Q}$ and $\mathbf{P}$ are orthogonal vectors arranged in order of the corresponding singular value. The columns of $\mathbf{Q}$ are called the left singular (or latent) vectors of $\mathbf{X}$, and $\mathbf{Q}$ is uniquely determined in as much as it is linearly related (ie by a diagonal matrix factor) to the eigenvectors of $\mathbf{X}\mathbf{X}^t$, and is identical following normalization. The columns of $\mathbf{P}$ are called the right singular (or latent) vectors of $\mathbf{X}$, and are the eigenvectors of $\mathbf{X}^t\mathbf{X}$, and are not uniquely determined (Horn and Johnson, p414 1985). The required transformation matrix $\mathbf{Q}$ (4.8) can then be uniquely determined from a direct decomposition of the data matrix $\mathbf{X}$ (4.9). The singular value decomposition (4.9) can be computed by a number of methods [2].

In the case of pattern classification using multiple pattern classes, a feature selection based on a K-L expansion of the mixture covariance matrix will not necessarily enhance or preserve class separability. One possibility is to incorporate *a priori* class probability into the definition of covariance (Chien and Fu, 1967), but a fundamentally better approach is to obtain the subspace mapping which maximises a crite-

---

[2] The SVD may be computed by a plane rotation method (Forsythe and Henrici, 1960), by an application of the QR algorithm (Wilkinson and Reinsch, 1971 p134; Businger and Golub, 1969), and also by iterative gradient methods (Haimi-Cohen and Cohen, 1987).

rion of class separability (Foley and Sammon 1975; Fukunaga and Mantock 1983).

Methods of dimensionality reduction by orthogonal projections related to the K-L expansion have been applied in speech processing. For example, in speech coding (Atal, 1983), and in speech recognition based upon *subspace methods* (Oja, 1983). These methods classify pattern vectors using a decision rule based upon discriminant functions (see section 5.2.1), but in a class-specific subspace of the original feature space, designed to optimize pattern discrimination. The optimal subspaces may be found using a supervized learning approach given by Kohonen (1979).

Two closely related techniques which are concerned with the inter-dependence of a group of variables are *principal components analysis* (PCA) and *factor analysis* (FA). The principal components are uncorrelated linear combinations of the original variables which are independent and also have extremal values of variance. In fact it is the property of stationary values of variance which is used to constrain the formulation of PCA. As a result, the first (most principal) component has the largest possible variance of any linear combination, while the last (least principal) component has the smallest. As we shall see in Chapter 5, the principal components are the eigenvectors of the sample covariance matrix describing the distribution of multivariate data in the feature space. The eigenvalues are the variances of this distribution along the respective principal axes. The K-L expansion of a zero-mean signal is entirely equivalent to a PC analysis of multivariate data. We have seen that the first few axes in the transformed space, the first few eigenvectors corresponding to the largest eigenvalues, account for most of the total variance, and that the system can be described more parsimoniously by them. However it should be pointed out that the final decision as to how many variables to discard is a subjective decision. An additional shortcoming is that the principal components are not invariant to the scale of the original measurements.

In factor analysis, instead of searching for a linear transformation of the variables into uncorrelated variables with stationary values of variance, we assume a model in which there are $m < n$ transformed variables, all with zero mean and unit variance. Where PCA is a linear transformation of the covariance matrix of a sample of multivariate data, FA is a linear model of the covariance structure. This model depends upon a factor model of the data

$$x = \Lambda y + \epsilon \tag{4.10}$$

where x is an n-vector of measurement data, and y is an m-vector, $m < n$, of "common factors" of x. These common factors are independent random variables which are normally distributed with zero mean and unit variance. The $n \times m$ matrix Λ contains "factor loadings", such as λ_{ij} which weights the jth common factor in the ith variable of x. The n-vector ϵ contains "latent factors", which are zero mean random variables such as e_i, which contributes specifically to the variance of the ith variable in x. With the variances of the latent factors collected into a diagonal matrix Ψ, such that $\psi_i = \text{var}(e_i)$, then from the variance of the ith variable in x

$$\sigma_{ii} = \sum_{j=1}^{m} \lambda_{ij}^2 + \psi_i \tag{4.11}$$

and the covariance between the ith and jth variables

$$\sigma_{ij} = \sum_{k=1}^{m} \lambda_{ik}\lambda_{jk} \tag{4.12}$$

we can construct a model of the correlation matrix

$$\mathbf{R}_m = \mathbf{\Lambda}\mathbf{\Lambda}^t + \mathbf{\Psi}. \qquad (4.13)$$

We note that $\mathbf{R}_m$ is *not* the sample covariance matrix, but is a matrix of variances and covariances specific to an m-factor model.

There is a similarity between FA (4.13) and PCA (4.5) in that both are linear and both rely upon matrix factorization. The factors in PCA are orthogonal, but FA is somewhat more general in that the factors need not be orthogonal. This results in the inherent dimensionality reduction of FA, and bypasses the shortcomings of PCA in feature selection. However, whereas for PCA the factorization has a unique solution, being constrained to extremal values of variance, for FA there may be any number of possible $\mathbf{\Lambda}$ matrices. Therefore some criterion for selecting a particular $\mathbf{\Lambda}$ is required, and this is typically an extremal "measure of parsimony" based upon the distribution of the factor loadings (Morrison, 1978 p324).

The factor analysis problem is to find $\mathbf{\Lambda}$, and using (4.11) find $\mathbf{\Psi}$, for an *a priori* given number of common factors m. The solution is based upon maximum likelihood estimation and is not so straightforward as for PCA. A necessary assumption is that the measurement data is non-singular and normally distributed. We estimate the factor parameters from the sample covariance matrix, using an expression for the likelihood of the sample covariance. The likelihood function, for example the Wishart density, is maximized in the parameters by forming the set of maximum likelihood equations $\partial L(\mathbf{\Lambda}, \mathbf{\Psi})/\partial\psi_i = 0$, $i = 1,\ldots,m$, and these are subsequently solved using an iterative numerical procedure to obtain the parameters of the m-factor model (Morrison, 1978 p308).

Still another technique for explaining inter-dependence amongst a set of variables is that of multi-dimensional scaling. This technique is basically a topological approach which aims to find a subspace of the measurement space which preserves the metric distance relationships between the items in a sample of multivariate data. The reader is referred to one of the recent texts on multivariate analysis, such as Seber (1984).

4.3. Feature extraction from speech patterns

In the case of speech patterns the usual approach is to assume *a priori* a speech production model, upon which the feature extraction transformation can be based. Feature extraction is then the transformation of the speech signal into vectors of speech parameters, such as the LP coefficients described in Chapter 3.

An alternative transformation is to directly extract the harmonic components of the signal by Fourier analysis, using the well known FFT algorithm. The appeal of this approach is that it models to some extent the function of the cochlea, which is known to analyse the speech signal into its harmonic components, to be fed down individual fibres of the auditory nerve into the brain.

A similar kind of transformation can also be done using a bank of band-pass filters, each tuned to a specific frequency band. This method has the advantage that the filter bank can be configured to have the characteristics of an *auditory model* (Lyon, 1982; Seneff, 1985). Such a model is designed to achieve similar input-output characteristics to the cochlea and associated auditory organs.

The principal disadvantage of FFT analysis, and the output from a reasonably detailed auditory model, is that the data is not reduced. We have simply achieved an intermediate representation, of similar dimensionality, in which the harmonic content of the signal is made explicit. It is then necessary to extract features from this intermediate representation, to produce pattern vectors of lower dimensionality.

This intermediate representation can be displayed as a *speech spectrogram* so that we can see the harmonic content of a speech signal. A spectrogram is a three-dimensional

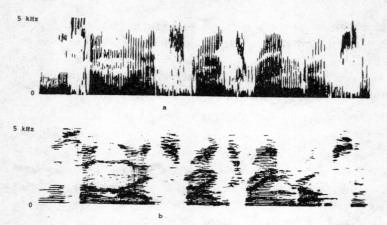

Figure 4.1. Spectrograms
"when the sunlight strikes rainbows on..."
(a) wideband spectrogram (b) narrow band spectrogram

pattern in which each point represents the magnitude of a particular frequency component at a particular time. The traditional form of a spectrogram as a pattern on paper derives from the way such patterns were originally produced, and is a frequency versus time plot in which magnitude is represented by the boldness of each plotted point, as in Figure 4.1. The spectrogram is also often displayed as a line drawing as in Figure 4.6.

The spectrogram is rich in information which characterizes auditory quality, and this can be directly related back to the state of the articulators in speech production, and so to a phonetic categorization of the speech sound. For example, in Figure 4.1a we can clearly see the dark patch of high-frequency noise during the unvoiced fricative /s/ in "sunlight" and "strikes". We can see vertical white bands of silence when there is a complete closure, such as during the stops /t/ and /k/. During the vowels we see a characteristic horizontal patterning, and the horizontal bands, such as can be seen during the vowel in "sun" in Figure 4.1a are called *formants*. The formants are caused by resonances inside the vocal tract, when driven by glottal pulses during voiced speech. The particular frequencies which resonate inside the vocal tract depend upon its size and shape, and therefore the formant frequencies can be related back to the shape of the vocal tract, and so to a phonetic categorization of vowel sounds.

Stationary vowels can be classified according to the values of the principal formants, usually the first three formants, which are denoted F_1, F_2, and F_3. For example, the vowel in "sun" typically has the first three formants at roundabout 500 Hz, 1000 Hz, and 2300 Hz respectively. The formant frequencies define a *vowel space* in which particular classes of vowel are represented by particular regions. If the formant frequencies for a number of utterances of a particular vowel are measured they can be seen to cluster in a characteristic region of the vowel space. From the viewpoint of pattern classification, we wish these characteristic regions to be compact for each class of vowel, and that the regions for different classes are well separated. In general the separation of pattern classes in the vowel space of F_1, F_2, and F_3 is not sufficient for reliable discrimination of all the vowels defined by phoneticians, if we wish to classify the vowels produced by a range of speakers. Various normalizations are possible (Nearey, 1978) with the aim of improving vowel discrimination, for example some normalization for vocal tract size is possible using the vowel sub-space F_1, $F_2 - F_1$, and $F_3 - F_1$.

The dipthongs are non-stationary vowel sounds, and can be seen in the spectrogram as *formant trajectories* which represent the changing shape of the vocal tract, as can be seen in Figure 4.1a during the vowel in "rain".

Much can be learned from a study of spectrograms. With practice it is possible actually to read the display. In a famous experiment (Cole, Rudnicky, Zue and Reddy, 1980) Zue was able to transcribe speech spectrograms directly into a sequence of phonetic symbols. It is significant to note that he was able to do this reliably without using any higher-level constraints such as a particular vocabulary and word syntax. The point of this experiment is that it demonstrates that this intermediate representation, the speech spectrogram, contains the significant features for phonetic decoding, and furthermore makes them explicit.

A recognition approach based upon prominent spectrogram events depends upon the existence of invariant categories, the use of which is likely to minimize the structural variation which remains to be explicitly represented. Following Stevens and Blumstein (1981), in order to perceive a segment as a particular category the signal must contain a degree of relatively invariant primary information. A speaker must hit, or come sufficiently close to, certain target articulatory configurations in order to be intelligible. These targets are described by the domains of manner and place of articulation, and in turn by combinations of acoustic correlates. The secondary information, the joining material between targets, is also important for the correct identification of primary targets.

Recognition based upon sound categories is an attractive paradigm provided the variations in the complex of acoustic correlates are systematic and can be finitely represented. There is evidence that this is a strong possibility in spectrogram reading experiments (Cole *et al.* 1980), which show the adequacy of local spectral information for phonetic decoding. However the application of this kind of knowledge is deceptively simple. For example the classification of consonants is often based upon small-scale evidence, such as the rising F_1 associated with syllable initial consonants, voice onset times, and so forth. Such detailed information is difficult to extract without prior expectation.

The spectrogram reader's strategy can be interpreted very broadly as follows: look for the most prominent events first, then use these events, plus a knowledge of what to expect, to search for more subtle events. It is considered, for example, that the identification of syllabic nuclei, de-voicing, abrupt releases, and strong frication are events of fundamental importance to the spectrogram reader. Only after the identification of a syllabic nucleus, for instance, will the small-scale trajectory of formants be extracted. This suggests a paradigm for feature extraction from the spectrogram representation, in which prominent events are extracted first, and subsequent feature extraction is guided by an expectation for particular subtle, small-scale events which is built into a structural model. The space of all possible segmental events is partitioned in this way to contain the combinatorics of classification possibilities. However emphasis on prominent events must always be tempered by the difficulty of error recovery.

In this chapter we shall be concerned with the extraction of features from this intermediate representation, the speech spectrogram. We shall discuss the analysis-frame problem, which was briefly mentioned in Chapter 3, in relation to the generation of speech spectrograms, and describe a method of *pitch synchronous* spectral analysis for the generation of smooth spectrograms. Then we shall describe a method for the extraction of some primitive features representative of prominent events in the spectrogram, such as syllabic nuclei, onsets and offsets, de-voicing, abrupt releases, and strong frication. The prominent events which are extracted are essentially those which may be used by the spectrogram reader in making an initial broad interpretation of FFT-based spectrograms in terms of manner of articulation classes. We note that a broad interpretation into manner classes is a more modest goal than a detailed phonetic transcription, but one for which the classification procedures will be more robust and reliable, simply because the classes are more separated in the pattern space. In Chapter 6 we shall see the utility of manner classes in the construction of syllables and words. Throughout this chapter, the emphasis is on the reduction of data concomitant with the preservation of the relevant information.

4.4. Pitch synchronous spectral analysis

In this section the frame problem for short-time Fourier analysis of continuous speech is discussed, and a new peak-picking algorithm is described which operates on the time waveform, resulting in a facility to synchronize the frame position and size to that of local glottal energy peaks and local pitch period during voiced speech. It turns out that particular time waveform peaks are sufficient indicators of glottal energy peak position, in the sense that their position relative to that of local glottal energy peaks is sufficiently constant; the spectrogram produced by short-time Fourier analysis of frames centred on these peaks retains important detail while being significantly smoother on both time and frequency axes. The algorithm also produces a good voiced-unvoiced decision, and a pitch estimation. As a pitch extractor this compares favourably with the speed of the autocorrelation method and the quality of the SIFT algorithm.

4.4.1. The frame problem

The frame problem is illustrated in Figure 4.1 and Figure 4.2. The wide-band (short-frame) spectra show a good time resolution but a poor frequency resolution. The vertical striations in Figure 4.1a correspond to glottal energy pulses. These striations are at pitch frequency when the frame size is less than the pitch period, otherwise they represent an alias of the local pitch, depending upon how well the frame samples the glottal pulses. The narrow-band (long-frame) spectra show a good frequency resolution, but a poor time resolution. The horizontal striations in Figure 4.1b correspond to pitch harmonics. The frequency difference between these striations represents the local pitch frequency provided the frame size is greater than the pitch period, otherwise the frequency resolution under-samples the pitch harmonics. The frame problem is then the selection of an appropriate analysis frame which best preserves both time and frequency information.

A reasonable compromise of time and frequency resolution is to use fixed 10 ms frames, often called "centisecond"

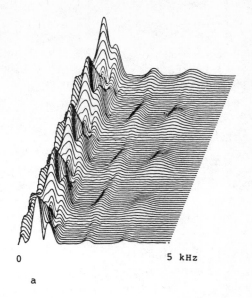

0   5 kHz

a

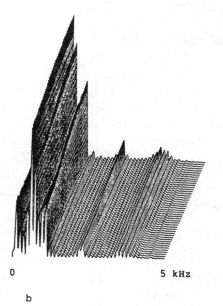

0   5 kHz

b

Figure 4.2. Spectrograms: high front vowel
(a) wideband spectrogram (b) narrow band spectrogram

frames, and in practice these are often overlapped by half a frame. An alternative idea is to use longer frames, and then smooth the resulting spectra to remove the pitch harmonics and reveal the formants. A common technique for spectral smoothing is that of cepstral filtering (Rabiner and Schafer, 1978). Here the discrete spectrum is taken as the input to a Fourier transform, and the resulting transform is known as a *cepstrum*. Periodic components in the spectrum, caused by pitch harmonics, will be represented by a distinct peak in the cepstrum. The smoothing process is achieved by detecting and removing this peak, and then applying the inverse Fourier transform to recover the original spectrum, now with the pitch harmonics removed.

The frequency resolution $\Omega = 1/NT$ [Hz], where N is the number of sample points per frame and T [Secs] is the sample interval of the time waveform, governs sampling in the frequency domain. As a minimum requirement to resolve the formants, $\Omega < F_1$, the first formant frequency. For an adequate time resolution of at least one pitch period, $\Omega \geq F_0$, the pitch frequency. A good compromise is $\Omega = F_0$, which has the additional advantage that pitch harmonics are not resolved. If $F_0 = 1/MT$, where M is the number of time samples within a local pitch period, then the best compromise is achieved by synchronizing the analysis frame size $N = M$. The effect of such a frame is to decouple the excitation component of the signal from the vocal-tract filter component. Provided the local pitch is not too high, the first and subsequent formants are resolved as well as possible in the spectra without resolving the pitch harmonics.

When time-evolving features are important it is necessary to synchronize the frame position as well as the frame size to the local glottal pulses. The procedure of short-time Fourier analysis conventionally samples data using a bell-shaped window, such as the Hamming window, in order to minimize the sidelobes of each channel response (Rabiner and Schafer, 1978). Consequently if the frame size is synchronized to the local pitch period, the energy sampled by the

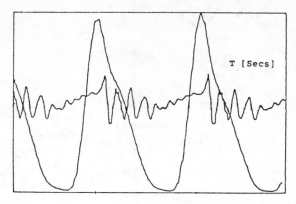

Figure 4.3. Frame energy as a function of frame position

frame varies according to the position of the frame relative
to the local glottal pulses. Figure 4.3 shows a detail of a
time waveform of voiced speech. Superimposed on this is the
low-frequency energy contour derived from 6.4 ms Hamming
windows. This window was shifted by single points along the
time waveform to generate each point on the energy contour.
The waveforms are aligned so that corresponding points are
in the centre of a frame. It can be seen that energy max-
ima occur in frames centred over peaks in the time waveform
which correspond to glottal peaks. If frame position is not
synchronized in this way, then spurious peaks and dips are
introduced into the energy contour, which may even come to
resemble features worthy of extraction.

By synchronizing the size and position of frames to the
local pitch period, the glottal pulses are exactly sampled in
the time domain, and the pitch harmonics in the frequency
domain. This is equivalent to extracting the envelope over
the glottal pulses and pitch harmonics, which results in a
smoother spectrogram on both time and frequency axes, and
achieves the maximum data reduction while preserving the
original spectrogram features.

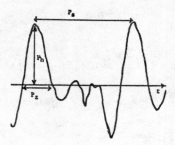

Figure 4.4. Simple peak measurements

4.4.2. A peak-picking algorithm

The proposed algorithm can be used to identify the time waveform peaks which best correspond to glottal energy peaks in voiced speech. The algorithm constructs a graph in which the vertices represent prominent waveform peaks and the edges represent links in a plausible sequence of glottal peaks. A cost function is given so that a dynamic programming search can find the minimum cost path through this graph, representing the most plausible sequence of glottal peaks. The glottal peaks can be used to synchronize Fourier analysis frames to the local pitch in the production of smooth spectrograms.

Initially simple peak measurements are used to identify and extract prominent peaks from the time waveform. The measurements made are shown in Figure 4.4. A waveform peak is defined as the highest (or lowest in the case of a valley) point between two zero crossings. Let S be the set of waveform peaks over a training set of speech data. Let S_g be the set of waveform peaks $S_g \subseteq S$ which best correspond to the position of glottal energy peaks. The set of "prominent" peaks, $S_p \subseteq S$, is defined $S_p = \{s(z, h) \mid z > Z, h > H\}$, where $s(z, h) \in S_p$ is a waveform peak (or valley), with zero-crossing separation z and height (or depth) h. The values of

Z and H are such that $|S_p|$ is a minimum with $S_g \subseteq S_p$. Approximations to Z and H are found experimentally by hand-labelling all the peaks $s(z,h) \in S_g$, and searching for the values of Z and H which minimize $|S_p|$ while $S_g \subseteq S_p$. The approximations to Z and H can be used to extract prominent peaks on-the-fly from the voiced speech signal. The set of prominent peaks S_p is a subset of all the waveform peaks which is guaranteed to include all the glottal peaks, and is small enough that the glottal peaks can be identified by a constrained search for glottal-peak sequences.

Peak sequences are represented by a graph constructed over the set of prominent peaks for each voiced stretch. The prominent peak extraction process identifies a voiced stretch as follows. Since $S_g \subseteq S_p$, a stretch of speech which contains no prominent peaks is un-voiced. Conversely a stretch of speech which contains a sequence of prominent peaks at a plausible pitch frequency is voiced. Isolated peaks or very short sequences may be regarded as un-voiced. In the peak sequence graph, paths which span the voiced stretch describe plausible sequences of glottal peaks. The particular sequence which best describes glottal peaks can now be found by searching the graph so as to minimize a cost function. The cost function is designed to rank the peak sequences on the assumption that the glottal sequence will contain the most prominent peaks with the smoothest amplitude and period variations.

The graph is constructed by assigning edges which link the prominent peaks so as to produce plausible sequences of glottal peaks. Let $S_p = s_1, \ldots, s_i, \ldots, s_N$ be the sequence of prominent peaks in a stretch of voiced speech. Let A_i be the amplitude of peak s_i, and T_{ij}, $j > i$, be the period between peaks s_i and s_j. Let the cost of a transition from peak s_i to peak s_j be

$$c_1(i,j) = \frac{|A_i - A_j|}{A_i + A_j} - \frac{A_i - a}{b - a} \qquad (4.14a)$$

97

where $a = \min_i A_i$ and $b = \max_i A_i$. Each term contributes a component in the interval $[0, 1]$. The minimum cost transition is between two peaks of similar high amplitude. Let the further cost of a transition from s_i to s_k via s_j be

$$c_2(i, j, k) = \frac{|T_{ij} - T_{jk}|}{T_{ij} + T_{jk}} \qquad (4.14b)$$

so that the minimum cost transition has the smallest period variation.

Let us briefly explain these cost functions. We wish a low cost to reflect the fact that the peak s_i is a large peak (second term in (4.14a)), that it has a similar amplitude to the next peak s_j (first term in (4.14a)), and that the period between s_i and s_j is similar to that between s_j and the following peak s_k (4.14b). This being the case we can use the accumulated cost of a sequence of peaks to rank the sequence, so that the minimum cost sequence contains the most prominent peaks with the smoothest amplitude and period variations, and this sequence is then most likely to be the sequence of glottal peaks. Each term in (4.14) is a mapping onto the interval $[0, 1]$, so as to normalize the respective components of peak cost. The second term in (4.14a) is simply a linear function $f: A_i \to [0, 1]$, with $f(a) = 0$ and $f(b) = 1$, to express a measure of relative peak amplitude, with the parameters a and b as the smallest and largest of all peak amplitudes respectively. The first term in (4.14a) and (4.14b) is slightly more complicated as there are two variables, however its effect becomes quite clear on examination of the partial differentials. These show that the mapping in this case is not linear, but it is designed so that the function is less sensitive to variations in its parameters when these parameters are larger values. So for example in the first term of (4.14a), when the peaks are large their relative difference needs to be correspondingly large to have an appreciable effect on the cost. This insensitivity to larger peaks compensates, in a somewhat *ad hoc* fashion, for the correspondingly larger random variations we would expect between the heights of larger peaks.

Path constraints over the graph are represented by functions which describe boundary conditions upon plausible peak sequences as follows:

$g_1(i,j)$ = 1 **if** 1. s_i and s_j are both peaks or dips.

         and 2. T_{ij} is a plausible pitch period.

         and 3. $|A_i - A_j| <$ max amplitude variation.

     $= \infty$ otherwise.

$g_2(i,j,k)$ = 1 **if** $|T_{ij} - T_{jk}| <$ max period variation.

          $= \infty$ otherwise.

$$(4.15)$$

Condition 3 for g_1 in (4.15) reflects the fact that voicing cannot start or stop abruptly, within one pitch period. The condition for g_2 describes the inherent bound on physically realizible pitch derivative due to muscular inertia.

On the basis of Bellman's principle of optimality it is possible to write the dynamic programming solution to the minimum cost path problem as:

$$C(i,N) = \min_{i<j<N} \left\{ c_1(i,j)g_1(i,j) + \right.$$

$$\left. \min_{j<k\leq N} \left\{ c_1(j,k)g_1(j,k) + c_2(i,j,k)g_2(i,j,k) + C(j,N) \right\} \right\}$$

$$0 < i < N - 1$$

$$(4.16)$$

where $C(i,N)$ is the cost of the minimum cost path through the graph between peaks s_i and s_N. The minimum cost path through the N peaks in S_p is then the path with cost $C(1, N)$, and the path itself, consisting of the sequence of glottal peaks, is determined by recording the path decision made at each peak during evaluation of the minimum cost. In the above formulation the peaks s_1 and s_N in S_p will always be considered glottal peaks, but if we assume the first and last glottal peaks will be amongst the first and last, say, three prominent peaks, then the minimum cost path is the smallest cost $C(m, n)$, for $m = 1, 2, 3$ and $n = N - 2, N - 1, N$.

Pitch contours can be generated by plotting the peak separations along the sequence of glottal peaks. Pitch synchronous spectrograms can be generated by centering each analysis frame over a glottal peak, with the size of each frame equal to the local peak separation.

During unvoiced speech, particularly at voiced/unvoiced boundaries, it is necessary to maintain the local trend in frame sizes to prevent the introduction of spurious discontinuities into the spectrogram. The frame sizes during unvoiced speech are based upon the sizes of the adjacent voiced speech frames. By fitting the frame sizes to a constrained arithmetic progression within the unvoiced interval, the frame sizes default to fixed values which vary smoothly between voiced intervals.

4.4.3. Results and Discussion

A sequence of three prominent peaks was found to be the minimum requirement for a decision on voicing, and with $Z = 0.5$ ms we obtained good voiced/unvoiced decisions. Figure 4.5 shows a comparison between pitch contours which illustrates the quality of the pitch tracking and of the voiced/un-voiced decision. The parameter H is not critical, its purpose being simply to discount waveform drift during quiet passages. Since all reasonable peak sequences are considered and ranked, the algorithm tends to find voicing if it exists. Local pitch derivatives were not tightly constrained so as to permit a certain amount of pitch "jitter". We have found that semi-voiced stretches invariably have at least one

Peak-picking method.
[see text]

SIFT algorithm.
[Markel 1972]

Autocorrelation method.
[Dubnowski et al. 1976]

Harmonic sieve.
[Duifhuis 1982]

["Did you see her on the ship"]   ["Joe took fathers shoe-bench out"]

Figure 4.5. A comparison of pitch contours

101

prominent peak or valley per pitch period, and the algorithm successfully classifies voiced fricatives and nasals as voiced. A common problem with pitch extraction is the pitch halving or doubling effect. The algorithm assigns a poor rank to peak sequences with a high relative peak-amplitude cost, and this provides a rejection of the pitch doubling effect. In the peak sequence graph, the deletion of edges which span periodic sub-sequences of peaks rejects the peak halving effect. In the case of high-pitched speech the frames become rather short, and to prevent the formants becoming smeared we generally default to a frame size of twice the local pitch period.

The principle advantage of this algorithm is that it identifies the position of the glottal peaks on the basis of sequence constraints as opposed to local peak constraints. Methods based upon local constraints (Gold and Rabiner, 1969) are susceptible to sporadic halving and doubling of the pitch period. The use of dynamic programming to search for the optimal peak sequence in terms of the given criteria is a means of rejecting local errors by making global decisions.

Figure 4.6 shows a comparison between a fixed-frame (10 ms frames) spectrogram with a pitch synchronous spectrogram, for the same utterance. The frame size is synchronized to the local pitch period, and this minimizes pitch harmonics in each spectrum. The frame position is centred over local glottal pulses so as to sample the speech during periods of maximum excitation. As a result the formants are sharp and distinct. The spectra are relatively wideband with correspondingly good time resolution, and the synchronized frame position minimizes ripple on energy contours in the time direction. Figure 4.7 shows the same data as Figure 4.6, following a 2-dimensional median smoothing process. When applied to the fixed-frame data, the smoothing process averages the random variations present in the pattern, resulting in a marked loss of information. Because the pitch-synchronous spectra contain less variation of a random nature, the resulting smoothed spectrogram retains the important information relevant to vocal-tract shape.

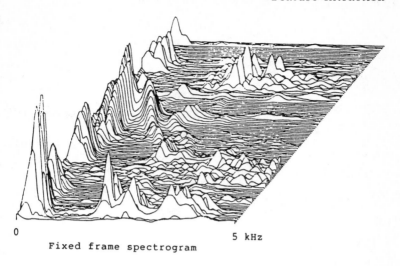

0   5 kHz

Fixed frame spectrogram

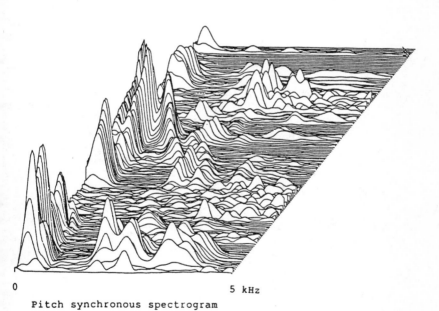

0   5 kHz

Pitch synchronous spectrogram

Figure 4.6. A comparison of spectrograms
"did you see her on the ship"
(a) fixed frame spectrogram (b) pitch synchronous spectrogram

103

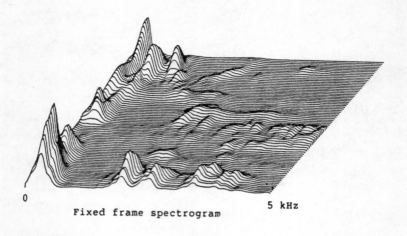

Fixed frame spectrogram

0   5 kHz

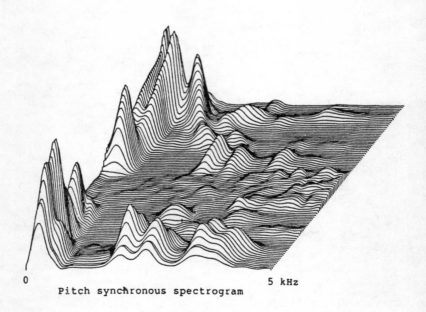

Pitch synchronous spectrogram

0   5 kHz

Figure 4.7. A comparison of smoothed spectrograms
"did you see her on the ship"
(a) fixed frame spectrogram (b) pitch synchronous spectrogram

The peak-picking algorithm as presented reliably produces better Fourier spectrograms at relatively small time overhead. In the worst case of failure of the voiced/un-voiced decision a temporary default to fixed frames as described does not impair spectrogram quality.

4.5. Spectrogram feature extraction

The smooth spectrogram obtained by pitch synchronous analysis is an intermediate representation of the speech signal, and we now consider feature extraction from the spectrogram to obtain pattern vectors for subsequent sequential classification.

Algorithms for formant tracking (McCandless, 1974) will not be discussed here. Instead we will describe a simple approach based upon the segmentation of time waveforms which are contours of constant frequency over the spectrogram. Amongst the simplest and most prominent features which can be extracted from the spectrogram are the segmental events which lie along a time-evolving spectral energy contour. A spectral energy contours is derived from a frequency band $f_2 - f_1$ over a spectrogram $[F_{kt}]_{m \times n}$ of $t = 1, \ldots, n$ time frames, each with $k = 1, \ldots, m$ discrete frequency channels. The contour is defined for a band $f_2 - f_1$ as

$$w_t = \frac{1}{|a - b|} \sum_{k=a}^{b} F_{kt} \quad , \quad t = 1, \ldots, n \qquad (4.17)$$

where

$$a = \frac{2m}{f_s} f_1 \quad , \quad b = \frac{2m}{f_s} f_2$$

and f_s is the sampling frequency in the time domain. Figure 4.8 shows two such contours at low and high frequency bands, with $f_1 = 200$, $f_2 = 800$, and $f_1 = 4700$, $f_2 = 5000$

105

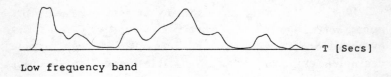

Low frequency band

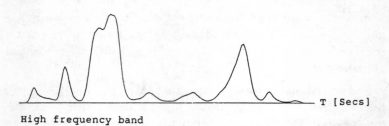

High frequency band

Figure 4.8. Energy contours
"did you see her on the ship"
(a) low frequency band (b) high frequency band

Hz respectively. The low bandwidth of the high-frequency information seems at odds with what is known about the auditory transformation of the speech signal, in particular that the frequency resolution falls off towards the higher end of the auditory band. However there is a good empirical reason for this, which is simply that frication energy should be separated from overall spectral energy, especially during sonorant peaks. With a higher sampling rate, the high frequency band could be usefully extended.

The low-frequency contour provides information to locate syllabic nuclei, onsets, offsets, and unvoiced regions. In the high-frequency contour the relevant events are periods of frication and bursts. Such events represent distinctive and informative pattern primitives which are shown in Chapter 6 to provide numerous cues to the manner of articulation. The next section describes an algorithm for the segmentation of these contours into significant primitive spectral *events*.

4.5.1. Waveform segmentation by hierarchical linear regression

A number of algorithms for waveform segmentation have been reported, principally in the areas of picture recognition and handwritten script recognition (Rosenfeld and Kak, 1976; Pavlidis, 1978). Line segments are often suggested as primitives, with each segment characterized by the locations of its end-points, its length, and slope. The problem of locating straight line segments on a waveform is not trivial. A simple approach based upon turning-points is inadequate because it ignores significant discontinuities in the slope of the waveform. A better piecewise linear approximation is obtained from the second derivative of the waveform (Marr, 1982); peaks in the second derivative indicate waveform discontinuities. Methods based upon peak identification suffer in general from a dependency upon the threshold used to define a peak. It is necessary to devise an algorithm which is relatively insensitive to threshold variation.

An interesting approach proposed by Witkin (1983) is to pick peaks in the second derivative of the waveform over a succession of different scales or resolutions. A majority decision then selects peaks which indicate a waveform discontinuity detectable over a range of scales. Distributing the peak-picking problem over a range of scales effectively reduces the sensitivity to particular thresholds.

The algorithm proposed here achieves a similar end by different means. The algorithm identifies prominent line segments over a hierarchy of line segmentations, generated by an agglomerative hierarchical clustering procedure (Späth, 1982). The inter-segment similarity criterion is a measure of segment co-linearity, and the measure used here is the least squared error of the y-on-x regression line.

The line of regression of y-on-x is the line $y = a + bx$ through a set of points (x_i, y_i), $i = 1, \ldots, n$, such that the sum of squared vertical deviations

$$d = \sum_{i=1}^{n}(y_i - a - bx_i)^2 \qquad (4.18)$$

is a minimum. In this sense the line is considered a "best fit" to the set of points. The parameters of this line are found using the familiar least-squares technique of differentiating (4.18) and forming the normal equations $\partial d/\partial a = 0$ and $\partial d/\partial b = 0$, which are solved simultaneously to obtain the regression line parameters a and b (Bajpai *et al.* 1978):

$$a = \bar{y} - b\bar{x} \qquad (4.19a)$$

$$b = \frac{\sum_{i=1}^{n}(x_i - \bar{x})(y_i - \bar{y})}{\sum_{i=1}^{n}(x_i - \bar{x})^2} \qquad (4.19b)$$

where $\bar{x}$ and $\bar{y}$ are the respective mean values of x_i and y_i for all the points $x_i, y_i, \ i = 1, \ldots, n$. The error of this regression line is used instead of the correlation coefficient when the x-axis is considered an indexing axis with values $1, 2, 3, \ldots, n$ which samples the waveform $y_1, y_2, y_3, \ldots, y_n$. Since $x_i = i, \ i = 1, \ldots, n$, the least-squares error (4.18) is

$$d = \sum_{i=1}^{n}(y_i - a - ib)^2 \qquad (4.20)$$

The formulas for the parameters (4.19) can also be simplified using the standard results:

$$\sum_{i=1}^{n} i = \frac{n(n+1)}{2} \qquad (4.21a)$$

$$\sum_{i=1}^{n} i^2 = \frac{n(n+1)(2n+1)}{6} \qquad (4.21b)$$

$$\sum_{i=1}^{n}(x_i - \bar{x})(y_i - \bar{y}) = \sum_{i=1}^{n} x_i y_i - \frac{\sum_{i=1}^{n} x_i \sum_{i=1}^{n} y_i}{n} \qquad (4.21c)$$

$$\sum_{i=1}^{n}(x_i - \bar{x})^2 = \sum_{i=1}^{n} x_i^2 - \frac{(\sum_{i=1}^{n} x_i)^2}{n} \qquad (4.21d)$$

from which it is easily shown that:

$$\bar{x} = \frac{n+1}{2} \qquad (4.22a)$$

$$\sum_{i=1}^{n}(x_i - \bar{x})(y_i - \bar{y}) = \sum_{i=1}^{n} i y_i - \frac{n+1}{2}\sum_{i=1}^{n} y_i \qquad (4.22b)$$

$$\sum_{i=1}^{n}(x_i - \bar{x})^2 = \frac{n(n+1)(n+5)}{12} \qquad (4.22c)$$

The parameters of the regression line (4.19) are then easily obtained from the quantities $\sum_{i=1}^{n} i y_i$ and $\sum_{i=1}^{n} y_i$.

The segmentation algorithm begins, at level 1, with n points of the waveform w_t (4.17) partitioned into n singleton sets which are segments, $S_1 \ni w_1, \ldots, S_n \ni w_n$. At level 2, the points are partitioned into $n - 1$ segments, at level 3 into $n - 2$ segments, and so on. At the kth level there are $n - k + 1$ segments, and a segment S_j, $1 \leq j \leq n - k + 1$, contains an ordered set of $|S_j|$ successive points from w_t. The algorithm procedes to construct a hierarchy of partitions from level 1 to each successive level by merging two adjacent segments into one. At each level the most "similar" pair of segments S_j, S_{j+1} are merged. The similarity of segments here is a measure of their co-linearity, and this is expressed as the minimization of a distance $d(S_j, S_{j+1})$. The steps in the algorithm are essentially as follows:

0. **Let** S_j be one of n ordered singleton segments at level $k = 1$.

1. **While** $k < n$

   1.1 Find $\operatorname{argmin} d(S_j, S_{j+1})$.

   1.2 Merge segments S_j and S_{j+1}, to form a new S_j from $S_j \cup S_{j+1}$.

   1.3 Delete segment S_{j+1}.

   1.4 $k = k + 1$.

The distance $d(S_j, S_{j+1})$ is defined as the error of the least-squares regression line through the points in $S_j \cup S_{j+1}$. From (4.20),

$$d(S_j, S_{j+1}) = \sum_{i=1}^{l} (y_i - a - ib)^2 \qquad (4.23)$$

where $l = |S_j| + |S_{j+1}|$ and y_i, $i = 1, \ldots, l$, is the ordered set of points in $S_j \cup S_{j+1}$. The parameters a and b are computed from (4.19) using (4.22).

The complexity of this segmentation algorithm is derived in terms of the number of times (4.23) is computed during the course of the algorithm. Rather than compute $\operatorname{argmin} d(S_j, S_{j+1})$ at every level of the algorithm, it is far more efficient to compute (4.23) once whenever a merge produces a new segment S_j. The cost may then be inserted into an ordered list of costs and associated arguments, so that $\min_j d(S_j, S_{j+1})$ is always at the head. The complexity is then equal to the number of merge operations, merge (S_j, S_{j+1}), excepting the final segment S_N, $N = n - k + 1$, for which S_{N+1} is undefined. The operation $\operatorname{merge}(S_{N-1}, S_N)$ occurs on average once whenever the remaining number of segments is halved, which is $\log_2 n$ times for n initial waveform points. Therefore over n levels, with one merge per level except the top,

$$\text{complexity} = n - 1 - \log_2 n \qquad (4.24)$$

This is an upper bound, reached when the waveform is entirely merged. The algorithm is actually arranged to halt before this is reached, at a threshold for an initial segmentation into "prominent" linear segments.

4.5.2. Segment prominence

Each level of the algorithm presents a particular *scale* of segmentation, from the initial fine scale (high resolution segmentation) of n segments at level 1, to the final coarse scale (low resolution segmentation) of 1 segment over the entire waveform at level n.

During execution of the algorithm, segments "grow" from the most linear regions of the waveform out towards regions of changing slope. Segment coalesce over the least significant non-linear regions first, so that the most prominent waveform discontinuities remain segment boundaries over the greatest range of levels. The result is a prominence hierarchy of segment boundaries, as shown in Figure 4.9.

Figure 4.9 shows the segment boundaries over a waveform in a succession of levels. It can be seen that any given segment is the root of a binary tree of the segments which have been successively merged in lower levels. Thus there is a mapping from the structure of segments shown in Figure 4.9 onto a binary tree of segments. This tree represents the alternative segmentations over a succession of resolutions, with the most prominent segments near the root. As a data structure this has the particular advantage that any non-singleton segment is the root of a hierarchy of sub-segments. Levels of structural detail within a segment, each with an implicit prominence ordering, are then easily accessible to the segment.

The selection of a particular segmentation from this hierarchy is based upon the fact that the cost incurred by a segment merging at each level, $\min_j d(S_j, S_{j+1})$, grows at a non-linear rate, and that the rate of change of this growth has a distinct maximum when "prominent" segments are merged. Figure 4.10 shows the cost of merging plotted against levels in

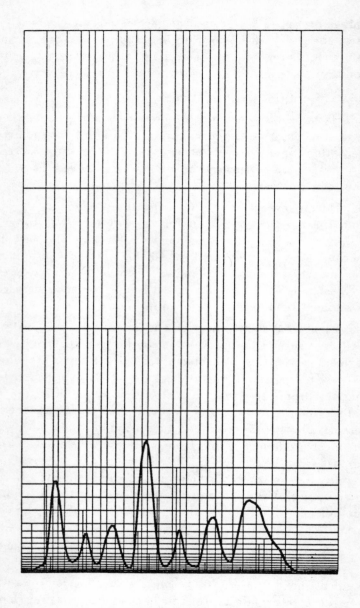

Figure 4.9. Segment prominence hierarchy
"bipity bopity boo"

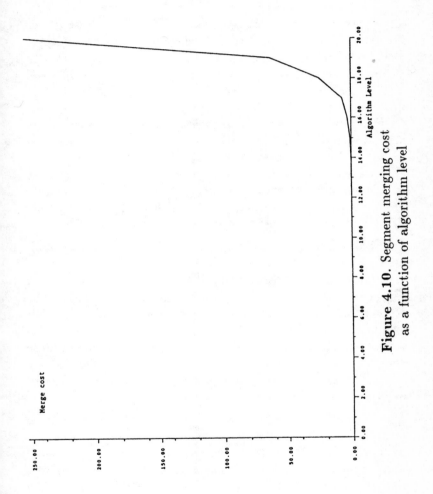

Figure 4.10. Segment merging cost
as a function of algorithm level

113

the algorithm for the utterance shown in the dendrogram of Figure 4.9. The point of maximum curvature in Figure 4.10 is the point at which the most prominent segments begin to be merged, and this point corresponds to the level of segmentation of the low frequency-band contour shown in Figure 4.11. This maximum in the rate of change of merging cost is easily detected and is used to halt the algorithm at a level k so that the segments $S_1, \ldots, S_{n-k+1}$ are the most prominent segments, in the sense of being the most linear segments over a range of scales. The point of maximum curvature in Figure 4.10 is typical of this kind of waveform, and represents a turning point between segmentation at high resolution and segmentation at low resolution. In this sense the segmentation shown in Figure 4.11 is significant, and is a natural choice for initial segments. The algorithm has been tested on a large number of waveforms of this kind, and consistently produces an initial segmentation which is remarkably close to a hand-segmentation into straight line segments.

The purpose of this segmentation is to delimit prominent spectrogram events so that feature extraction can be specialized. The segmentation of the low-frequency contour reveals events such as syllabic onsets, peaks, and offsets. The segmentation of the high-frequency contour makes explicit events such as noise bursts, which may accompany the release from a stop consonant such as /t/, and sustained noise produced by a fricative consonant such as /s/. The feature extraction process is then to make measurements at each segment so as to produce a sequence of pattern vectors.

To motivate the selection of features we will assume *a priori* a speech production model which generates spectrogram events, of the type we can segment, using a knowledge of articulatory phonetics. Thus we can assume, for example, that the duration of a syllabic peak is a significant feature in vowel discrimination, that the rate of onset to a syllabic peak is significant to initial consonant discrimination, and so forth. Each pattern vector is then a set of measurements which characterize a segment and which provide a complex

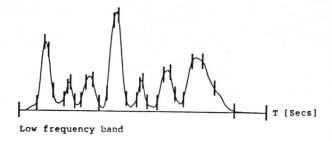

Low frequency band

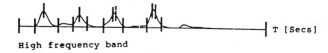

High frequency band

Figure 4.11. Segmentation of energy contour
"bipity bopity boo"
(a) low frequency band (b) high frequency band

of acoustic cues. When a sequence of pattern vectors is subsequently classified, these acoustic cues are directly related back to the state of the phonetic speech-production model, and so to a broad phonetic categorization.

The classification of pattern vectors is described in the next chapter, and in Chapter 6 we will develop a phonetic speech-production model in terms of a simple set of features extracted from these segments of spectral energy contours.

CHAPTER 5

A composite pattern recognition model for speech features

5.1. Introduction

In this chapter the pattern recognition model described in Chapter 2 is re-formulated using continuous probability density functions instead of fuzzy set membership functions in order to take advantage of standard clustering and parameter estimation techniques. The model is based upon an augmented context-free grammar, including qualitative descriptions of feature variations, in which to formulate structural linguistic knowledge. The structural components of a pattern are qualified, as in Chapter 2, by parametric functions which partition the feature spaces associated with the pattern components. Given the qualified description, the corresponding quantitative constraints may be learned from observations of data by a parameter estimation procedure.

The proposed model is a cross or hybrid of pattern-matching and knowledge-based approaches. The advantages of a pattern matching approach, namely a well-formulated algorithm utilizing a principle of constrained optimization, are augmented by *a priori* knowledge of the structural constraints inherent in speech and language. Primitive features are classified as pattern components with an associated degree of belief. This degree of belief is the basis of evidential reasoning amongst the alternative structural interpretations of the primitive components. The decisions made during recognition are optimal in the maximum likelihood sense, with respect to the training data.

The chapter begins with a review of the methods of vector-space pattern recognition. These methods are the basis of pattern matching.

5.2. Vector-space pattern recognition

A model of vector space pattern recognition usually consists of three parts: a transducer for signal acquisition and digitization, a feature extractor which performs a signal analysis and/or transformation from measurement data to pattern data in the form of feature vectors x, and a classifier which assigns the feature vectors to one of a finite number of classes ω_i, $i = 1, \ldots, m$.

A pattern primitive is represented by n features, $x = (x_1, \ldots, x_n)^t$. A useful interpretation of this n-dimensional feature vector is as a point in an n-dimensional feature space. For example Figure 5.1 shows two pattern classes in a 2-dimensional feature space. Each point is a 2-measurement observation. The figure shows one plausible linear decision boundary between the classes.

A sample of feature vectors from a particular class of pattern will tend to cluster in a characteristic region of the feature space, while a sample from another class will tend to cluster in a different region. The approach to classification is basically one of partitioning the feature space into regions, one region for each class of pattern, by selecting decision boundaries according to some criterion of optimality, depending upon the methodology chosen. An important common factor in the range of techniques available for this purpose is that the partitions can be estimated directly from observations of training data. The techniques vary in the representation of these partitions, but each one offers some kind of optimality criterion for the partitions and the decision

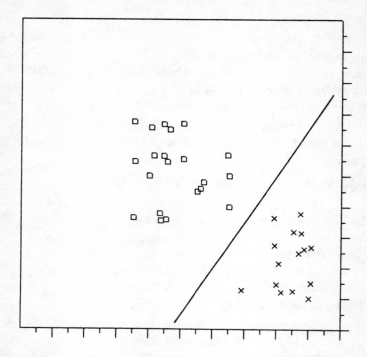

Figure 5.1. Two pattern classes in a 2D space

rules which operate to classify unknown pattern vectors. The techniques broadly divide into three methodologies (Levinson, 1985a) which are referred to as geometric, topological, and probabilistic.

5.2.1. Geometric decision rules

The geometric approach operates by estimating the parameters of an optimal partition function on the feature space, according to class-separability criteria. The decision rule classifies vectors by their position with respect to the partitions. Initially we assume a form of *discriminant function*, and then estimate its parameters from the data. There are various training procedures, some statistical and some not, but in all cases these procedures don't require a knowledge of the underlying probability distributions, and in this sense they are non-parametric.

In the simplest case we assume a discriminant function associated with pattern class ω_i, $D_i(x)$, which is a linear combination of the elements of x,

$$D_i(x) = w_i^t x + w_{i0} \qquad (5.1)$$

where w_i is a weight vector, and w_{i0} is the threshold weight associated with class ω_i. All feature vectors which satisfy the equation $D_i(x) = 0$ lie in a hyperplane, with orientation specified by w_i, which is normal to the hyperplane, and with location specified by w_{i0}. For any feature vector x the function $D_i(x)$ is proportional to the signed distance from x to the hyperplane. Therefore the hyperplane divides the feature space into two, forming a decision surface, with $D_i(x) > 0$ for all vectors on one side of the hyperplane, and $D_i(x) < 0$ for all vectors on the other side.

This decision surface can be used to classify a feature vector x by positioning a hyperplane between pairs of classes, ω_i and ω_j. To do this we need to estimate the weights w_i, w_{i0}, w_j, and w_{j0}, such that all vectors which satisfy the equation $D_i(x) - D_j(x) = 0$ lie in the hyperplane which best separates ω_i from ω_j. Given these weights, then all x for which $D_i(x) - D_j(x) > 0$ lie on the ω_i side of the hyperplane, and all x for which $D_i(x) - D_j(x) < 0$ lie on the ω_j side. This can be generalized as the multi-class decision rule:

assign x to ω_i if $D_i(x) > D_j(x)$ for all $j \neq i$ classes $\quad (5.2)$

The training procedure for linear classifiers is then to estimate the weights associated with each class, so as to obtain the best set of discriminant functions, according to some criterion of optimality.

For example, if the classes are linearly separable, then the best discriminant plane is that which optimizes a criterion function $J(w_i)$, which expresses the combined distance

119

from all points $x \in \omega_i$ to the hyperplane $D_i(x) = 0$. Given a function $J(w_i)$, such as the perceptron criterion (Rosenblatt, 1961), the solution vector w_i can be obtained by a gradient descent or relaxation procedure, which incrementally modifies w_i until it converges onto a solution for which $J(w_i)$ is minimized (Nillson, 1965).

If the classes are not linearly separable, then alternative criteria based upon least squared errors can be used. In this case the vector w_i has a closed-form solution by the familiar technique of least-squares parameter estimation.

In general the training procedure aims to solve the set of inequalities $w_i^t x > 0$, using a set of training feature-vectors $x_j^{(i)}$, $j = 1, \ldots, N_i$, for classes ω_i, $i = 1, \ldots, m$. The approaches can be broadly divided into those which are deterministic, such as the perceptron algorithm (Rosenblatt, 1961) and the least mean-square algorithm (Ho and Kashyap, 1965), and those which are statistical, such as the methods of stochastic approximation exemplified by the Robbins-Monro algorithm (Robbins and Monro, 1951), and the method of potential functions (Aizerman *et al*, 1964). Various criterion functions and minimization procedures with convergence proofs are described by Duda and Hart (1973).

The geometric approach to pattern classification using linear discriminant functions is applicable when the classes are linearly, or piecewise linearly separable. It is particularly appropriate when decision surfaces can be used to partition pattern classes which do not have a natural clustering property. However pattern classes are not always cleanly separable by partition functions, linear or otherwise, and when the classes have a clustering property in one or more modes then non-linear class boundaries can be found more simply using one of the following methods.

5.2.2. Topological decision rules

When the pattern classes have a distinct clustering property in the feature space, then perhaps the simplest and most intuitive approach to classification is to classify a pattern according to its proximity to the pattern classes. This proximity is a pattern-to-class distance measure defined in terms of the metric distance between a feature vector and the prototypical cluster of points in the feature space which are characteristic of a particular class. Given a distance measure $D(x, \omega_i)$, between pattern vector x and the class ω_i, $1 \leq i \leq m$, then the decision rule of minimum distance pattern classification is:

$$\text{assign } x \text{ to } \omega_i \text{ if } D(x, \omega_i) < D(x, \omega_j) \\ \text{for all } j \neq i \text{ classes} \tag{5.3}$$

The distance measure $D(x, \omega_i)$ is defined in terms of a metric $d(x, y)$ on the feature space, which is a generalized distance measure of the point-to-point distance between vectors x and y. The choice of a distance metric depends upon the application, and is inevitably a trade-off between computational complexity and performance in the task of pattern discrimination. We shall consider various metrics and their properties presently.

The form of the distance measure $D(x, \omega_i)$, in terms of the metric, depends upon the way the pattern classes cluster in the feature space. If each class ω_i tends to cluster tightly around a single prototypical point, the class mean vector $\mu^{(i)}$, then $D(x, \omega_i)$ may be defined as the simple point-to-point distance,

$$D(x, \omega_i) = d(x, \mu^{(i)}) \tag{5.4}$$

If each class tends to cluster in K modes, so that a class ω_i can be represented by K_i prototypical points $\mu_j^{(i)}$, $j = 1, \ldots, K_i$, then the point-to-class distance may be defined:

121

$$D(\boldsymbol{x}, \omega_i) = \min_{1 \leq j \leq K_i} d\left(\boldsymbol{x}, \boldsymbol{\mu}_j^{(i)}\right) \tag{5.5}$$

If the pattern classes do not cluster sufficiently well to be represented by prototypical points, then a more general measure of point-to-class distance may be used, such as a K-nearest-neighbour (K-NN) rule.

For the K-NN rule, each class ω_i, $i = 1, \ldots, m$, is represented by a set of known points in the feature space, so that a class ω_i is represented by N_i points, $z_j^{(i)}$, $j = 1, \ldots, N_i$. There are various forms of K-NN rule, but in all types the first step is to sort the distances, $d\left(\boldsymbol{x}, z_j^{(i)}\right)$, for each class. This sorting procedure makes a K-NN list $\boldsymbol{y}_j^{(i)}$, $j = 1, \ldots, N_i$, for each class ω_i, $i = 1, \ldots, m$, and each list is ordered such that $d\left(\boldsymbol{x}, \boldsymbol{y}_j^{(i)}\right) \leq d\left(\boldsymbol{x}, \boldsymbol{y}_{j+1}^{(i)}\right)$. The simplest K-NN rule then defines the distance to the Kth nearest neighbour in class ω_i,

$$D(\boldsymbol{x}, \omega_i) = d\left(\boldsymbol{x}, \boldsymbol{y}_K^{(i)}\right) \tag{5.6}$$

Another K-NN rule defines the distance as the average distance of $\boldsymbol{x}$ to the K nearest neighbours in ω_i:

$$D(\boldsymbol{x}, \omega_i) = \sum_{j=1}^{K} d\left(\boldsymbol{x}, \boldsymbol{y}_j^{(i)}\right) \tag{5.7}$$

The factor $1/K$, usually required to form an average, is unnecessary here from the viewpoint of the decision rule (5.3). Still another K-NN rule is based upon a majority decision as to which class is most represented in the first K members of a merged K-NN list, consisting of the ordered point-to-point distances irrespective of class. The distance is then

$$D(\boldsymbol{x}, \omega_i) = \frac{1}{\min_i l_i} \tag{5.8}$$

where l_i is the number of points in the first K members of the merged list which are associated with class ω_i.

The distance measure $D(x, \omega_i)$ is defined in terms of a metric $d(x, y)$ on the feature space, which is a generalized distance measure obeying certain axioms of Euclidean distance:

(i) $d(x, y) \geq 0$ and $d(x, y) = 0$ iff $x = y$.

(ii) $d(x, y) = d(y, x)$

(iii) $d(x, y) \leq d(x, z) + d(z, y)$

so that a metric is a point-to-point distance between vectors x and y which is (i) non-negative, (ii) symmetric, and (iii) the shortest distance between two points in the metric space (the triangle inequality).

Metrics may be broadly divided into linear metrics, which measure distance equally in all directions, and non-linear metrics, which weight the distance depending upon its direction in the feature space.

The linear metrics are defined in terms of the $L_p(n)$ norm of an n-vector, which can be thought of as a generalized measure of the length of the vector,

$$\|x\|_p = \left(\sum_{i=1}^{n} |x_i|^p \right)^{1/p} \tag{5.9}$$

The metric defined on this norm is called the Minowski metric,

$$d(x, y) = \|x - y\|_p = \left(\sum_{i=1}^{n} |x_i - y_i|^p \right)^{1/p} \tag{5.10}$$

which, by vector subtraction, is a generalized measure of the distance between the vectors x and y. The well known special cases of this metric are $p = 1$, $p = 2$, and $p = \infty$, which respectively define:

The Hamming or city-block metric:

$$d(\boldsymbol{x}, \boldsymbol{y}) = \|\boldsymbol{x} - \boldsymbol{y}\| = \sum_{i=1}^{n} |x_i - y_i| \tag{5.11}$$

The Euclidean metric:

$$d(\boldsymbol{x}, \boldsymbol{y}) = \|\boldsymbol{x} - \boldsymbol{y}\|_2 = \left[(\boldsymbol{x} - \boldsymbol{y})^t (\boldsymbol{x} - \boldsymbol{y}) \right]^{1/2}$$

$$= \left(\sum_{i=1}^{n} |x_i - y_i|^2 \right)^{1/2} \tag{5.12}$$

The Chebychev metric:

$$d(\boldsymbol{x}, \boldsymbol{y}) = \|\boldsymbol{x} - \boldsymbol{y}\|_\infty = \max_{1 \leq i \leq n} |x_i - y_i| \tag{5.13}$$

The non-linear metrics of most practical interest are quadratic metrics, defined in general terms as the quadratic form:

$$d(\boldsymbol{x}, \boldsymbol{y}) = (\boldsymbol{x} - \boldsymbol{y})^t \mathbf{A} (\boldsymbol{x} - \boldsymbol{y}) = \sum_{i=1}^{n} \sum_{j=1}^{n} \mathbf{A}_{ij} (x_i - y_i)(x_j - y_j) \tag{5.14}$$

where $\mathbf{A}$ is an $n \times n$ positive-definite real symmetric matrix. We note that when $\mathbf{A}$ is diagonal, this reduces to the weighted inner product $\sum_{i=1}^{n} \mathbf{A}_{ii}(x_i - y_i)^2$. A quadratic form of particular interest, as will be seen later, is the squared Mahalanobis distance,

$$d(\boldsymbol{x}, \boldsymbol{y}) = (\boldsymbol{x} - \boldsymbol{y})^t \mathbf{C}^{-1} (\boldsymbol{x} - \boldsymbol{y}) \tag{5.15}$$

where $\mathbf{C}$ is the sample covariance matrix describing the likely distribution of the set of vectors of which $\boldsymbol{y}$ is typical.

In some cases, non-metric distance measures may be more appropriate, such as the non-metric distance function

$$d(x, y) = \frac{\|x - y\|}{\|x + y\|} \qquad (5.16)$$

or the non-metric similarity function

$$s(x, y) = \frac{x^t y}{\|x\|_2 \|y\|_2} \qquad (5.17)$$

This function expresses the cosine of the angle between the vectors, and is a maximum when they have the same orientation. The function (5.16) is a multivariate version of the weighted distance (4.14b) used in the peak-picking algorithm. Another example of a useful non-metric distance measure is the Itakura distance (3.15) between vectors of LP coefficients of speech data.

The essential difference between the linear and quadratic metrics can be seen by comparing the Euclidean squared norm $x^t x$ with the weighted Euclidean squared norm $x^t A x$. For the linear norm, the locus of points which satisfy the equation $x^t x = r^2$, where r is constant, is spherical in n-dimensions, centred at the origin, and with radius r. For the quadratic norm, the corresponding locus for $x^t A x = r^2$ is ellipsoidal in n-dimensions, centred at the origin. The orientation and eccentricity of this ellipsoid depend upon the matrix A. If A is diagonal, so that the elements $a_{ij} = 0$ when $i \neq j$, then there are no mixed terms in the equation, and the principal axes of the ellipsoid are aligned with the coordinate axes of the feature space. The diagonal elements are then scaling factors, so that the radius along the ith principal axis is $r/\sqrt{a_{ii}}$. In the case of $A = I$, the unit matrix, the quadratic reduces to linear form. Symmetric elements off the diagonal in matrix A contribute weight to the mixed or correlated terms, and cause a rotation of the ellipsoid about the origin.

For both linear and quadratic norms, the transformation $x^* = x - y$ simply translates the origin to the point y, and for a given x and y the norm is then the metric distance between x and y. The loci described above are then contours of constant distance, and we see that where the linear metrics measure distance equally in all directions, the quadratic metrics weight distance according to its direction, and that the scaling and rotation are dependent upon the elements a_{ij} of the matrix $\mathbf{A}$.

The quadratic norm is an important description of intra-class distance as a result of the central limit theorem which shows that the distribution of vectors x in the feature space, which belong to a particular class, tend to be normal[1]. Suppose that a stationary random process generates feature vectors x which are normally distributed in the feature space. Each vector is a multivariate random variable, and the distribution of a sample of vectors is characterized by the mean vector μ and the covariance matrix $\mathbf{C}$ (the multivariate versions of the mean and variance which characterize a uni-variate normal distribution). The standard multi-normal variate is $(x - \mu)^t \mathbf{C}^{-1} (x - \mu)$ (which is the multivariate version of the standard normal variate $(x - \mu)^2 / \sigma^2$), so that the standardized distribution has zero mean and unit variance. We see that the normal distribution of sample vectors in the feature space is ellipsoidal. The orientation and eccentricity of this ellipsoid depend upon the elements of the covariance matric $\mathbf{C}$, and again this can be seen as the scaling and rotation of a sphere in n-dimensions. The scaling is the result of differences in the natural variance of each variable in x, and also any differences in the scales of measurement used for each variable. The rotation is the result when the variables in x are not statistically independent; when there is some correlation between the variables.

---

[1] We assume that a pattern class is represented by a constant signal, or prototypical value, but observations of the signal are corrupted by additive zero-mean white noise. Observed deviations from the signal have a Gaussian distribution.

In topological decision rules there may be simple cases when a linear metric distance $d(x, \mu)$ is sufficient to discriminate between pattern classes. But this distance clearly takes no account of the ellipsoidal shape of a class distribution, which will generally be an important factor in any measure of the proximity of a vector to a pattern class. To account for the ellipsoidal shape of the class distribution, the local probability structure, we have two options: we can either use a quadratic metric such as the Mahalanobis distance ((5.15), with C the sample covariance matrix for the class and y its mean vector), or we can use a linear metric on a suitably transformed (normalized) space. We shall see the quadratic and linear metrics are identical through a transformation which maps an ellipsoidal distribution onto a space where it is spherical. To show this we will again use the norms $x^t x$ and $x^t A x$ for convenience, noting that the origin can easily be translated to any point in the feature space. We will show that $x^t A x = y^t y$, when $y = Tx$ where T is a non-singular matrix, and the matrix A is factored such that $A = T^t T$. We will then show that the matrix T can be obtained from the principal components, the eigenvectors and eigenvalues, of the matrix A, in a very useful form which explicitly separates the rotation and the scaling components of the transformation.

The positive-definite real symmetric matrix A is called a *Gram matrix*, and is an important concept in multivariate statistics, where it represents a generalized covariance. Any Gram matrix can be factored as $A = T^t T$, where T is a non-singular $n \times n$ matrix (Basilevsky, 1983 p137). Substituting this into the quadratic form we have

$$
\begin{aligned}
x^t A x &= x^t T^t T x \\
&= (Tx)^t T x \\
&= y^t y, \quad \text{with } y = Tx.
\end{aligned}
$$

Therefore the quadratic distance $x^t A x$ equals the Euclidean distance $y^t y$ following the transformation $y = \mathbf{T}x$. When the matrix $\mathbf{A}$ describes the orientation and eccentricity of a class distribution then both these distances have the same normalising property which accounts for the ellipsoidal shape of the distribution.

The factorization $\mathbf{A} = \mathbf{T}^t \mathbf{T}$ is not unique, but we can find a particular transformation matrix $\mathbf{T}$ which is information preserving and has two distinct effects: a rigid rotation which diagonalizes matrix $\mathbf{A}$, and a scaling which reduces the diagonalized matrix to the unit matrix. It is of course possible to diagonalize $\mathbf{A}$ using an *equivalence transformation* of simple row and column operations, but the resulting diagonal matrix is not necessarily a *similarity transformation*, in that the information on the ellipsoidal shape of the class, contained in $\mathbf{A}$, is not fully preserved. To preserve this information, the direction components of the rotation must span the entire feature space; in other words these components must be orthogonal. The required similarity transform is an orthogonal rotation which aligns the principal axes of the ellipsoid with the coordinate axes of the feature space, followed by a scaling which reduces the rectilinearly oriented ellipsoid to a sphere in n-dimensions.

To locate the principal axes of the ellipsoid we need to locate *optimal values* which are points on the surface of the ellipsoid with extremal distance from the centre. We also note that each optimal value shares a common tangent with a sphere $x^t x = r^2$. Therefore we can use the method of Lagrange multipliers to optimize x in order to maximize $x^t \mathbf{A} x$ under the constraint that x also lies on the sphere $x^t x = r^2$. Let the vectors x which lie on the common tangent points of ellipse and sphere be q_i, $i = 1, \ldots, n$. Then if λ_i is a Lagrange multiplier,

$$\phi = q_i^t \mathbf{A} q_i - \lambda_i (q_i^t q_i - r_i^2).$$

Differentiating with respect to q_i and setting to zero we have

$\partial\phi/\partial q_i = \mathbf{A}q_i - \lambda_i q_i = 0$, from which the characteristic equation is

$$(\mathbf{A} - \lambda_i \mathbf{I})q_i = 0 , \quad i = 1,\ldots,n.$$

The solutions to this set of equations are the eigenvectors [2] q_i, $i = 1,\ldots,n$, which are optimal values on the surface of the ellipsoid, and their corresponding eigenvalues [3] λ_i, each of which is a radius of the ellipsoid along the principal axis through the centre of the ellipsoid and the respective optimal value. There are a number of algorithms available for computing the eigenvectors and eigenvalues of a positive definite real symmetric matrix [4]. With the λ_i collected as the elements of a diagonal matrix $\mathbf{\Lambda}$, and the vectors q_i as the columns of an $n \times n$ orthogonal matrix $\mathbf{P}$, the characteristic equation is written $\mathbf{AP} = \mathbf{P\Lambda}$, and when $\mathbf{P}$ is normalized for unit length, by dividing each q_i by r_i^2, we have an orthonormal or unitary matrix for which $\mathbf{P}^t\mathbf{P} = \mathbf{I}$, so the characteristic equation can be written

$$\mathbf{A} = \mathbf{P\Lambda P}^t. \tag{5.18}$$

This is called the *spectral decomposition* [5] of $\mathbf{A}$. In general any Gram matrix $\mathbf{A}$ can be uniquely factored as $\mathbf{A} = \mathbf{P\Lambda P}^t$,

---

[2] The eigenvectors are also known as the latent vectors, the characteristic vectors, or the principal components.

[3] The eigenvalues are also known as the latent roots, the characteristic values, or the singular values.

[4] See (Faddeev and Faddeeva, 1963), and (Wilkinson and Reinsch, 1971), or (Golub and Van Loan, 1983) for theory and description, and see (Businger, 1965) for a program listing to compute the eigenvalues and eigenvectors of a real symmetric matrix. Better still, use well-tested routines from one of the major packages, such as EISPACK (Smith *et al*, 1970) or LINPACK (Dongarra *et al*, 1978).

[5] The spectral decomposition of a Gram matrix is a canonical reduction which is a special case of the singular value decomposition (see Section 4.2). The spectral decomposition is related to the

where $\mathbf{P}$ is the matrix of normalized column eigenvectors, and $\mathbf{\Lambda}$ is the diagonal matrix of the corresponding eigenvalues.

The spectral decomposition of $\mathbf{A}$ provides the unique factorization of $\mathbf{A}$ with the required information preserving properties. To put it in the form $\mathbf{A} = \mathbf{T}^t\mathbf{T}$, we factor $\mathbf{\Lambda}$ into $\mathbf{\Lambda} = \mathbf{W}^t\mathbf{W}$, where $\mathbf{W}$ is a diagonal matrix with elements such that $w_i = \sqrt{\lambda_i}$, so that

$$
\begin{aligned}
\mathbf{A} &= \mathbf{P}\mathbf{\Lambda}\mathbf{P}^t \\
&= \mathbf{P}\mathbf{W}^t\mathbf{W}\mathbf{P}^t \\
&= (\mathbf{W}\mathbf{P}^t)^t\mathbf{W}\mathbf{P}^t \\
&= \mathbf{T}^t\mathbf{T}, \quad \text{with } \mathbf{T} = \mathbf{W}\mathbf{P}^t.
\end{aligned}
$$

The transformation $y = \mathbf{T}x$, with $\mathbf{T} = \mathbf{W}\mathbf{P}^t$, is then the required similarity transformation which effects an orthogonal rotation using $\mathbf{P}$, followed by scaling using $\mathbf{W}$, such that the ellipsoidal class distribution is spherical in the transformed space. It is then appropriate to use a metric based on the linear norm $y^t y$ to measure the pattern-to-class distance.

We will now consider some special cases, and the first of these is the quadratic norm $x^t\mathbf{C}^{-1}x$, where $\mathbf{C}$ is the covariance matrix describing a class distribution. In Section 5.2.3 we shall see this matrix must also be positive definite. By the spectral decomposition theorem, $\mathbf{C}^{-1} = (\mathbf{P}\mathbf{\Lambda}\mathbf{P}^t)^{-1} = (\mathbf{P}^t)^{-1}\mathbf{\Lambda}^{-1}\mathbf{P}^{-1}$, where the matrices $\mathbf{P}$ and $\mathbf{\Lambda}$ are as defined, but for the covariance matrix $\mathbf{C}$. Matrix $\mathbf{P}$ is orthonormal, so that $\mathbf{P}^{-1} = \mathbf{P}^t$ and $(\mathbf{P}^t)^{-1} = \mathbf{P}$, and so $\mathbf{C}^{-1} = \mathbf{P}\mathbf{\Lambda}^{-1}\mathbf{P}^t$. With $\mathbf{\Lambda}^{-1}$ factored as $\mathbf{\Lambda}^{-1} = (\mathbf{W}^{-1})^t\mathbf{W}^{-1}$, we have by similar means the transform $\mathbf{T} = \mathbf{W}^{-1}\mathbf{P}^t$. So we see the squared Mahalanobis distance $(x - \mu)^t\mathbf{C}^{-1}(x - \mu)$ equals the squared Euclidean distance $y^t y$ when $y = \mathbf{T}(x - \mu)$

---

spectral density function in that, for example, the eigenvalues of a signal autocovariance matrix are equally spaced samples of the signal power spectrum (Wise, 1955).

and $\mathbf{T} = \mathbf{W}^{-1}\mathbf{P}^t$, and both these distances account for the ellipsoidal shape of the class distribution described by the covariance matrix $\mathbf{C}$. We note that each eigenvalue λ_i of the covariance matrix equals the variance of the marginal probability distribution along the ith principal axis. The Mahalanobis metric is often referred to as a *scale invariant* metric because it accounts for the shape of the class distribution directly, without requiring a transformation of the variables in $\boldsymbol{x}$, and is literally invariant to changes in the scales of measurement of the variables. The spectral decomposition of the covariance matrix provides the link between the topological methods of pattern classification and the probabilistic methods described in the next section, and is also the underlying mechanism used in principal components analysis and in the Karhunen-Loéve expansion described in Chapter 4.

The second special case is that of pure orthogonal rotation. Under the transformation $\boldsymbol{y} = \mathbf{P}^t\boldsymbol{x}$, the quadratic norm $\boldsymbol{x}^t\mathbf{C}^{-1}\boldsymbol{x}$ can be reduced to $(\mathbf{P}\boldsymbol{y})^t\mathbf{C}^{-1}\mathbf{P}\boldsymbol{y} = \boldsymbol{y}^t\mathbf{P}^t\mathbf{C}^{-1}\mathbf{P}\boldsymbol{y} = \boldsymbol{y}^t\boldsymbol{\Lambda}^{-1}\boldsymbol{y}$. The orthogonal transformation $\mathbf{P}^t\boldsymbol{x}$ is a rigid rotation which leaves all intra-class distances unchanged. The principal axes of the class distribution are rotated into alignment with the coordinate axes of the feature space, so that the ellipsoidal shape of the class can be described by the diagonal matrix $\boldsymbol{\Lambda}$. This effectively decouples the variables in each vector $\boldsymbol{x}$, so that they are uncorrelated in the transformed space. In addition the computation of the quadratic form reduces to a weighted inner product. We note that each eigenvalue $\lambda_i = \sigma_i^2$, the variance of the ith independent variable in $\boldsymbol{y}$.

The last special case is that of pure scaling. In general a scaling transformation $\boldsymbol{y} = \mathbf{T}\boldsymbol{x}$ can use any diagonal matrix $\mathbf{T}$ to weight each variable in $\boldsymbol{x}$. This weighting is usually designed to normalize the shape of the class distribution, by accounting for the variances. Under the transformation $\boldsymbol{y} = \mathbf{W}^{-1}\boldsymbol{x}$, with matrix $\mathbf{W}$ as defined, the squared Euclidean distance accounts for an approximation to the el-

131

lipsoidal shape of the class distribution. The values λ_i in the matrix $\mathbf{W}$ are derived from the principal components of the distribution, but are applied to scale it at the coordinate axes of the feature space. Although the scale factors are correct, they are applied in the wrong orientation, and hence the transformed distribution is not spherical. However this approximation may be perfectly adequate if the variables in x are "nearly" independent. If that is the case, then a simpler scaling transformation may also be adequate, in which $\mathbf{W}$ is defined as the diagonal matrix of the sample standard deviations, σ_i, of each variable in x. The scale factors and their orientation are now both approximations, but if the distribution is already close to a rectilinear orientation, then it will be "nearly" spherical in the transformed space. Using this approach, the distance computations are relatively simple, and we do not need to calculate the eigenvalues. However, for a reasonable approximation, the variables must be nearly uncorrelated, and their respective standard deviations should not differ greatly in value. This transformation is applied locally to each pattern class, using sample statistics derived from a set of training vectors for each class. Before a clustering procedure identifies the modes of each class, it is a good idea to apply a global scaling transformation in which $\mathbf{W}$ is defined as the diagonal matrix of the sample standard deviations of each variable in all training vectors irrespective of class. Such a transformation normalizes the scales of measurement of each variable over the entire training set, so that each variable has unit standard deviation.

In the remainder of this section we discuss the training procedure for topological decision rules, and describe measures of classifier performance from the viewpoint of multiclass discrimination, in terms of distance measures of pattern class separation in the feature space. The training procedure for topological decisions is a cluster analysis of training data. Such a procedure can be used to identify plausible classes of pattern in a training set, as in vector quantization, or if the classes are known *a priori* then cluster analysis is a *super-*

vized learning procedure which identifies the modes of the pattern class distributions. The *modes* of a pattern class are one or more prototypical points, or mean vectors, about which feature vectors will tend to form distinct clusters.

In general, a cluster analysis procedure identifies clusters of pattern vectors in the feature space X_i, $i = 1, \ldots, k$, with the objective of maximally separating clusters X_i and X_j for all $i \neq j$. The appearance of gestalt clusters of vectors in the feature space depends upon the scales of measurement of the variables, and will radically change if the scale along one coordinate axis is varied. It is therefore necessary to normalize these scales of measurement, and this can be done as a prerequisite to the clustering procedure, or by the use of a suitable scale invariant metric during clustering. A training set of patterns is pre-processed by a global transformation, as described, so that the average covariance matrix of all vectors, irrespective of class, reduces to the unit matrix. The training set is then partitioned by assigning vectors to particular clusters. A cluster analysis procedure operates by incrementally modifying these cluster partitions so as to optimize an objective function. The objective function is some measure of the cluster separation in the feature space.

We will describe two objective functions based upon linear metrics. Following Fisher (1936) we can define linear objective functions in terms of scatter matrices.

Let the total scatter matrix $\mathbf{S}_T$ be the covariance matrix of all vectors irrespective of cluster:

$$\mathbf{S}_T = \mathrm{E}\left[(\boldsymbol{x} - \boldsymbol{\mu})(\boldsymbol{x} - \boldsymbol{\mu})^t\right] \qquad (5.19)$$

The intra (within) cluster scatter matrix is the average cluster covariance matrix:

$$\mathbf{S}_w = \frac{1}{k} \sum_{i=1}^{k} \left[\frac{1}{K_i} \sum_{j=1}^{K_i} \left(\boldsymbol{x}_j^{(i)} - \boldsymbol{\mu}^{(i)}\right)\left(\boldsymbol{x}_j^{(i)} - \boldsymbol{\mu}^{(i)}\right)^t \right] \qquad (5.20)$$

133

The inter (between) cluster scatter matrix can be defined:

$$S_b = \frac{1}{k} \sum_{i=1}^{k} \left(\mu^{(i)} - \mu\right)\left(\mu^{(i)} - \mu\right)^t \qquad (5.21a)$$

or

$$S_b = \frac{2}{k(k-1)} \sum_{i=1}^{k-1} \sum_{j=i+1}^{k} \left(\mu^{(i)} - \mu^{(j)}\right)\left(\mu^{(i)} - \mu^{(j)}\right)^t \; (5.21b)$$

where μ is the mean of all vectors irrespective of cluster, and there are k clusters X_i, each assigned K_i points $x^{(i)}$, with mean vector $\mu^{(i)}$. Using the fact that $\mathrm{tr}(xx^t) = x^t x$, where $\mathrm{tr}(\cdot)$ is the trace operation, we see that $\mathrm{tr}(S_w)$ is the average point-to-set Euclidean distance. The inter-cluster distance is then $\mathrm{tr}(S_b)$, being the average squared deviation of the cluster centroids from the population mean μ (5.21a), or the average pairwise centroid separation for $\frac{1}{2}k(k-1)$ pairs of cluster centroids $\mu^{(i)}$ and $\mu^{(j)}$ (5.21b). The objective function may then be defined as $J_1 = \mathrm{tr}(S_b)/\mathrm{tr}(S_w)$, the ratio of inter-cluster separation to intra-cluster dispersion, which is maximized for clusters which are optimally compact and well-separated. Alternatively, viewing the determinant of a symmetric matrix as volume, we can define the intra-cluster scatter as $|S_w|$, being a measure of the average volume occupied by the points within a cluster. An objective function which tends to favour an even distribution of clusters in the feature space is then $J_2 = |S_T|/|S_w|$.

Given an algorithm which partitions the training set of feature vectors into clusters to maximize an objective function J, the final value of J will be a measure related to the quality or performance of a classification procedure for assigning unknown vectors to pattern classes represented by the clusters. This performance index reflects to some extent the discriminating power of a pattern classifier based upon these clusters. The relative merits of particular variables can be assessed, for the purpose of feature selection (see Chapter 4), from the viewpoint of pattern discrimination. Certain variables, or combinations of covarying variables, may provide more discriminatory information than others. It is possible to weight these variables according to their significance in terms of this performance index, and also to discard variables which contribute insignificant information for pattern discrimination.

Despite the advantage of their relative simplicity, the topological objective functions described above provide only a rough indication of classifier performance. They are loosely related to the classification error probability in that they describe the relative proximity of clusters in the feature space, but they do not describe the extent of any overlap between clusters in close proximity. Again we see that objective functions based upon linear metrics are an approximation which takes no account of the local probability structure of the clusters. In order that the value of J be a reasonable indication of classifier performance, the clusters must have similar covariance matrices. Quadratic objective functions which take local probability structure into account, and are closely related to classification error probability, will be described in the next section as probabilistic distance measures.

There are various algorithms for clustering feature vectors (Späth, 1982) and one that is both simple and effective is the K-means algorithm. This is described as follows:

0. Partition the training set into k clusters.

1. Repeat until converged:

    1.1 Calculate cluster centroids $\mu^{(i)} = \frac{1}{K_i} \sum_{j=1}^{K_i} x_j^{(i)}$, $i = 1, \ldots, k$.

    1.2 Re-assign each point x to the nearest cluster to minimize

$$\left(x - \mu^{(i)}\right)^t \left(x - \mu^{(i)}\right), \text{ for } 1 \leq i \leq k.$$

The effect of step 1.2 is to minimize $\mathrm{tr}(S_w)$, and the algorithm converges to a steady value of this intra-cluster dispersion measure. The number of clusters k is given *a priori*, and the procedure is to try various k with the aim of maximising

the objective function J. The algorithm is only locally optimal (Späth, 1982), and the results are dependent upon the
initial partition, and so it is recommended to maximize J over
a number of initial partitions. An alternative formulation of
this algorithm, described by Späth (p70), uses recursive estimation to update the cluster centroids and intra-cluster distances as individual points are transferred between clusters.

In the general case of supervized learning using a cluster
analysis of m sets of training vectors, each known to belong to
a pattern class ω_i, $1 \leq i \leq m$, the aim is to find one or more
modes or distinct clusters representative of each class. Each
of the k clusters is one mode of a pattern class, with $k \geq m$,
so that it is necessary to decide *a priori* how many modes will
be used to represent each class during the clustering procedure. It is necessary to enumerate all the possibilities for distributing k modes amongst m classes, and each of these sets
of mode-to-class assignments will initiate a clustering procedure with step 0 of the above algorithm, by partitioning the
m-class training set into k modes, each assigned to a particular class. The number of ways k modes can be distributed
amongst m classes is $\binom{k-1}{k-m}$ and if the maximum number
of modes to be considered overall is K, then the clustering
procedure is required $\sum_{j=m}^{K} \binom{j-1}{j-m}$ times. With $K \gg m$ this
becomes a very large number, and so it is necessary to be con-
servative in the assignment of multiple modes. The procedure
for enumerating the sets of initial mode-to-class assignments
is constrained by the following conditions:

1. Every class must be represented by one or more modes.
2. No two classes are assigned the same mode.
3. No mode is un-assigned.

With $1 \leq i \leq m$ classes, and $1 \leq j \leq k$ modes, each set of
mode-to-class assignments can be represented by an $m \times k$
binary matrix $\mathbf{M}$, with elements $M_{ij} = 1$ if mode j is assigned to class i. The above constraints are embodied in the
following recursive procedure, in which each recursive descent
maintains its own copy of matrix $\mathbf{M}$.

1. **procedure** $A(i, j, M)$
    1.1 $M_{ij} = 1$
    1.2 **if** $i > 1$ **then** $A(i - 1, j - 1, M)$
    1.3 **if** $j > i$ **then** $A(i, j - 1, M)$
    1.4 **if** $j = 1$ **then** output (M).

Initially $M_{ij} = 0$ for all i and j, and the procedure is started with $A(m, k, M)$. The procedure generates $\binom{k-1}{k-m}$ matrices M, each of which represents one *a priori* decision as to the number of modes which will be used to represent each pattern class during the clustering procedure. Each matrix M is the basis for an initial k-fold partition, and the training set representative of each class is partitioned randomly into the respective number of modes assigned to it. The K-means algorithm may then be used to identify the optimal partitions. To maintain the integrity of the pattern classes during clustering, step 1.2 of the K-means algorithm described above is modified so that each point x is re-assigned to the nearest mode (ie cluster) of its class. If x is known to belong to class ω_i, then re-assign x to the nearest mode X_j for which $M_{ij} = 1$. The procedure of mode-to-class assignment followed by the K-means algorithm is repeated for $k = m, m + 1, \ldots, K$, resulting in the aforementioned number of possible clusterings of between m and K clusters. The final step is to select the best clustering according to an objective function as described.

Finally we will discuss the advantages and disadvantages of the topological methods described above with respect to the probabilistic methods to be described in the following section. The distinction between the use of linear and quadratic metrics can also be seen as the non-parametric and parametric dichotomy in classification methods. Non-parametric methods such as the topological methods essentially do not require a knowledge of the underlying probability distributions of pattern classes in the feature space. This can be a decisive advantage when there is insufficient training data to estimate adequately the parameters of the probability distributions, as the topological methods can still perform relatively well on small data sets. Parametric methods, which are described in the next section, require a sufficient quantity of training data to ensure that the sample parameters are reasonable estimates of the population parameters, and critically to ensure that there are no singularities in the probability distributions of the training data. The non-parametric methods are relatively simple to implement and to train. In particular, for the K-NN approach it may be adequate just to record a prototypical sample of training vectors. However, as pattern classifiers the non-parametric methods are generally more computationally intensive than parametric methods. With the overheads of the normalising transformations, and all the distance computations, the topological methods are slower in execution than probabilistic methods.

5.2.3. Probabilistic decision rules

The probabilistic decision rule assigns an unknown vector membership of the class of highest probability. The decision rule is based on the relative likelihood of a feature vector x in a pattern class ω_i, $1 \leq i \leq m$. In this approach the feature vectors are considered vectors of random variables which are distributed according to analytic probability density (likelihood) functions, the parameters of which can be estimated directly from observations of pattern data. Prior knowledge in a probabilistic sense can be incorporated into the decision rule by an application of Bayes theorem, as will be described.

First we review of the laws of probability in relation to pattern classes in the feature space. We will assume that at any particular instant in time, one pattern class ω_i, $1 \leq i \leq m$, will be the current "state of nature". The natural occurrence of a class ω_i is an event, and this has an associated probability, denoted $\Pr(\omega_i)$. The probability of an event is defined as the limiting relative frequency of its occurrence,

$$\Pr(\omega_i) = \frac{\mathrm{F}(\omega_i)}{N_s} \qquad (5.22)$$

where $F(\omega_i)$ denotes the frequency or number of times the class ω_i occurs in a sample of N_s observations of the "state of nature". The probability is simply the normalized frequency of an event, and is a real number in the interval [0,1]. An impossible event is assigned zero probability, and a certainty is assigned unit probability. Since at least one event in the sample space of pattern classes is a certainty,

$$\Pr(\omega_1 \cup \omega_2 \cup \cdots \cup \omega_m) = 1 \qquad (5.23)$$

where $\Pr(\omega_1 \cup \omega_2 \cup \cdots)$ denotes the probability of occurrence of ω_1 or ω_2, and so on. The probability of at least one of two events ω_1 and ω_2 is

$$\Pr(\omega_1 \cup \omega_2) = \Pr(\omega_1) + \Pr(\omega_2) - \Pr(\omega_1, \omega_2) \qquad (5.24)$$

where $\Pr(\omega_1, \omega_2)$ denotes the probability of occurrence of ω_1 and ω_2. At any instant the occurrence of pattern classes is mutually exclusive; just one pattern class is the true "state of nature", so that $\Pr(\omega_i, \omega_j) = 0$ for all $i \neq j$. The probability for the occurrence of one class from the first $k < m$ classes is

$$\Pr(\omega_1 \cup \omega_2 \cup \cdots \cup \omega_k) = \sum_{i=1}^{k} \Pr(\omega_i) \qquad (5.25)$$

Events not mutually exclusive have $0 \leq \Pr(\omega_i, \omega_j) \leq 1$. As an example of such events, consider pattern classes φ_1, φ_2, etc., which occur in sequence, one per successive time frame. If these events are statistically independent, the probability of the events φ_1 and φ_2 is

$$\Pr(\varphi_1, \varphi_2) = \Pr(\varphi_1)\Pr(\varphi_2) \qquad (5.26)$$

and the probability for k events in sequence is

$$\Pr(\varphi_1, \varphi_2, \ldots, \varphi_k) = \prod_{i=1}^{k} \Pr(\varphi_i) \qquad (5.27)$$

If the events are not independent, so that the occurrence of some class will influence the class which occurs next, then it is necessary to account for the dependence in terms of a conditional probability. The probability of the event φ_1 and φ_2 is then

$$\Pr(\varphi_1, \varphi_2) = \Pr(\varphi_1)\Pr(\varphi_2/\varphi_1) \qquad (5.28)$$

where $\Pr(\varphi_2/\varphi_1)$ denotes the probability for φ_2 conditioned on the occurrence of φ_1. Similarly the probability for k dependent events in sequence is

$$\begin{aligned}
\Pr(\varphi_1, \varphi_2, \ldots, \varphi_N) = \\
\Pr(\varphi_1)\Pr(\varphi_2/\varphi_1)\Pr(\varphi_3/\varphi_2, \varphi_1) \cdots \Pr(\varphi_k/\varphi_{k-1}, \ldots, \varphi_1) \\
= \prod_{i=1}^{k} \Pr(\varphi_i/\varphi_1, \varphi_2, \ldots, \varphi_{i-1})
\end{aligned}$$
$$(5.29)$$

where $\Pr(\varphi_k/\varphi_{k-1}, \ldots, \varphi_1)$ denotes the probability for the occurrence of φ_k conditioned on the occurrence of φ_{k-1} and φ_{k-2} and $\ldots$ φ_1. Another example of events which are not mutually exclusive but are dependent is the occurrence of a pattern class ω_i with the observation of a value x. (We will generalize this to include observations of feature vectors presently). The probability of both events is symmetrical in that $\Pr(\omega_i, x) = \Pr(x, \omega_i)$, and from (5.28) $\Pr(\omega_i)\Pr(x/\omega_i) = \Pr(x)\Pr(\omega_i/x)$, or

$$\Pr(\omega_i/x) = \frac{\Pr(\omega_i)\Pr(x/\omega_i)}{\Pr(x)} \qquad (5.30)$$

This is Bayes theorem of conditional probability, and it expresses the probability for the occurrence of class ω_i conditioned upon observation of value x. In other words, the probability that an event x, which is known to have occurred, was reached via an event ω_i, $1 \leq i \leq m$. Since it is certain that the event x was reached exclusively by some event ω_i, from (5.23) and (5.25) we see

$$\sum_{i=1}^{N} \Pr(\omega_i/x) = 1 \qquad (5.31a)$$

and from (5.30),

$$\Pr(x) = \sum_{i=1}^{N} \Pr(\omega_i)\Pr(x/\omega_i) \qquad (5.31b)$$

For most practical purposes the range of values which x may take precludes the use of discrete probabilities for $\Pr(x/\omega_i)$ and $\Pr(x)$, and instead we use the likelihood functions described below.

If an event such as the occurrence of a pattern class is associated to some degree with a range of mutually exclusive values $x_1, \ldots, x_N$, then the event can be described by a discrete probability distribution, $\Pr(x_1), \ldots, \Pr(x_N)$. For statistical *consistency* ((5.23) and (5.25)) we require that

$$\sum_{i=1}^{N} \Pr(x_i) = 1 \qquad (5.32)$$

If we now consider the probability density in the interval δx when the number of values N increases to infinity, the sum becomes an integral,

$$\int_{-\infty}^{+\infty} \mathrm{p}(x)\,dx = 1 \qquad (5.33)$$

where $p(x)$ is a probability density function of the continuous variable x. We may calculate the probability of x taking a value within some interval by setting particular limits on the integral (5.33). The value of $p(x)$ for a particular x is not a probability (the probability vanishes when the limits of (5.33) are equal), but can be thought of as a measure of the *likelihood* of a value x with respect to the event described by the density function. For example, if the event is a pattern class ω_i, then the class-conditional probability density function $p(x/\omega_i)$ expresses the likelihood of a value x in this class.

Using likelihood functions, Bayes rule is written

$$\Pr(\omega_i/x) = \frac{\Pr(\omega_i)p(x/\omega_i)}{p(x)} \qquad (5.34)$$

where $\Pr(\omega_i)$ is the *a priori* probability for the natural occurrence of class ω_i, and $p(x/\omega_i)$ is the class-conditional probability density function or likelihood that value x is observed in class ω_i, and $p(x)$ is the unconditional probability density function for all value observations in the feature space. We see that Bayes rule expresses a revised opinion, in which the *a priori* probability for the occurrence of class ω_i is revised upon observation of a value x, which has a known likelihood of occurrence in class ω_i, to form the *a posteriori* probability.

We now apply Bayes rule in a maximum *a posteriori* (MAP) decision rule, by which it is possible to assign an observed feature vector x membership of some pattern class ω_i, $1 \leq i \leq m$, with the minimum risk of error, provided all the underlying probability values are known. The decision is based upon the *a posteriori* probability $\Pr(\omega_i/x)$, which is the probability of class ω_i having observed vector x. The MAP decision rule is

$$\begin{array}{c} \text{assign } x \text{ to } \omega_i \text{ if } \Pr(\omega_i/x) > \Pr(\omega_j/x) \\ \text{for all } j \neq i \text{ classes} \end{array} \qquad (5.35)$$

This rule is justified, assuming there is no loss in being correct and all errors are equally costly, by the conditional risk

$$\sum_{j=1}^{m} \Pr(\omega_j/\boldsymbol{x}), \quad j \neq i \qquad (5.36)$$

which is clearly minimized when the maximum *a posteriori* probability is selected. The *a posteriori* probability is calculated using Bayes rule for multivariate data,

$$\Pr(\omega_i/\boldsymbol{x}) = \frac{\Pr(\omega_i)p(\boldsymbol{x}/\omega_i)}{p(\boldsymbol{x})} \qquad (5.37)$$

where $p(\boldsymbol{x}/\omega_i)$ is the multivariate class-conditional probability density function or likelihood that vector $\boldsymbol{x}$ is observed in class ω_i, and $p(\boldsymbol{x})$ is the unconditional probability density function for all observations in the feature space. From (5.31) we see that $p(\boldsymbol{x})$ serves as a normalising factor to ensure statistical consistency, but it plays no part in the decision-making process (5.35). Consequently an equivalent MAP rule can be formulated in terms of the *a priori* probability and the likelihood instead of the *a posteriori* probability,

$$\text{assign } \boldsymbol{x} \text{ to } \omega_i \text{ if } \Pr(\omega_i)p(\boldsymbol{x}/\omega_i) > \Pr(\omega_j)p(\boldsymbol{x}/\omega_j)$$
$$\text{for all } j \neq i \text{ classes} \qquad (5.38)$$

If we assume all classes are *a priori* equally likely to occur, then the decision rule is simply a comparison of the likelihoods. Bayes theorem provides a way of incorporating prior knowledge and expectation, in the form of *a priori* probabilities, into the decision process. We can estimate the *a priori* probabilities for each class from the relative frequencies of their occurrence, and for a given density function describing $p(\boldsymbol{x}/\omega_i)$ we can estimate the parameters from training observations of x known to belong to ω_i. Thus (5.38) is a pattern classification model based entirely upon observations of data and the form of the probability density function, and which is optimal with respect to these things in the sense of minimising the conditional risk or probability of classification error.

There are many forms of probability density function, each of which may be appropriate under particular circumstances. For example, if we make the reasonable assumption that a pattern class ω_i is represented by a prototypical vector μ_i, about which there may be random (zero-mean white noise) variations, then the distribution of vectors characteristic of this class is normal. Such a model is a good approximation of many natural processes, and consequently the normal or Gaussian density function is the most commonly used probability density function. The univariate normal density function is:

$$p(x) = \frac{1}{(2\pi)^{\frac{1}{2}}\sigma} \exp\left[-\tfrac{1}{2}\frac{(x-\mu)^2}{\sigma^2}\right] \qquad (5.39)$$

and this is the familiar bell-shaped curve with a maximum at $x = \mu$ and $p(x) = \frac{1}{(2\pi)^{\frac{1}{2}}\sigma}$. The function is completely specified by two parameters, the mean μ and the variance σ^2. For simplicity the normal density is often denoted $N(\mu, \sigma^2)$. The univariate function is generalized to describe distributions of feature vectors in an n-dimensional feature space by the multivariate normal density function:

$$p(x) = \frac{1}{(2\pi)^{\frac{n}{2}}|C|^{\frac{1}{2}}} \exp\left[-\tfrac{1}{2}(x-\mu)^t C^{-1}(x-\mu)\right] \qquad (5.40)$$

This function, denoted $N(\mu, C)$, is completely specified by the mean vector μ, which locates the distribution, and the covariance matrix $\mathbf{C}$, which describes the shape of the distribution. The parameters μ and $\mathbf{C}$ are estimated from a sample of training data, as will be described. The likelihood function $p(x/\omega_i)$ is the multivariate density $N(\mu_i, \mathbf{C}_i)$, with parameters estimated from a training sample of vectors known to belong to class ω_i. The function $p(x/\omega_i)$ then expresses the likelihood of vector x in class ω_i.

From the viewpoint of the MAP decision rule (5.38) it is more convenient to work with the natural logarithm of the likelihood function. The logarithm is a monotonic operation which does not affect the decision process, so the rule can be written

assign x to ω_i if $d_i(x) > d_j(x)$ for all $j \neq i$ classes   (5.41)

where $d_i(x) = \log \Pr(\omega_i) + \log p(x/\omega_i)$ and
$d_j(x) = \log \Pr(\omega_j) + \log p(x/\omega_j)$. Taking the natural logarithm of (5.40) for the likelihood $p(x/\omega_i)$ we have

$$\log p(x/\omega_i) = -\tfrac{1}{2}n \log 2\pi - \tfrac{1}{2} \log |\mathbf{C}_i| - \tfrac{1}{2}(x - \mu_i)^t \mathbf{C}_i^{-1}(x - \mu_i)$$
$$(5.42)$$

and since the term $-\tfrac{1}{2}n \log 2\pi$ is independent of the class we can write

$$d_i(x) = \log \Pr(\omega_i) - \tfrac{1}{2} \log |\mathbf{C}_i| - \tfrac{1}{2}(x - \mu_i)^t \mathbf{C}_i^{-1}(x - \mu_i) \quad (5.43)$$

with a similar result for $d_j(x)$. Since the first two terms are independent of x they can be pre-stored, so that only the quadratic form need be computed for each decision. This computation is further simplified when $\mathbf{C}_i$ is diagonal, as described in the previous section. In this case the feature measurements are completely uncorrelated, and since the inverse of a diagonal matrix is also diagonal, the quadratic form $(x - \mu_i)^t \mathbf{C}_i^{-1}(x - \mu_i)$ reduces to inner products.

We now consider the estimation of the parameters μ_i and $\mathbf{C}_i$ for each class ω_i, $1 \leq i \leq m$. The parameters will be estimated from a training sample of N feature vectors $\boldsymbol{x} = (x_1, \ldots, x_n)^t$ known to belong to class ω_i. The mean of each variable x_i in $\boldsymbol{x}$ is

$$\mu_i = \mathrm{E}\left[x_i\right] = \frac{1}{N} \sum x_i \tag{5.44}$$

where $\mathrm{E}[\cdot]$ is the expectation operator, and the summation is over all N vectors associated with class ω_i. The sample mean vector, describing the centroid of the sample, is defined

$$\boldsymbol{\mu} = \begin{pmatrix} \mu_1 \\ \vdots \\ \mu_n \end{pmatrix} = \mathrm{E}\left[\boldsymbol{x}\right] \tag{5.45}$$

The variance of each variable x_i in $\boldsymbol{x}$ is

$$\begin{aligned} \sigma_i^2 = \sigma_{ii} &= \mathrm{E}\left[(x_i - \mu_i)^2\right] \\ &= \mathrm{E}\left[x_i^2\right] - \mu_i^2 \end{aligned} \tag{5.46}$$

We note that the factor $\frac{1}{N}$ in the expectation may be replaced by $\frac{1}{N-1}$ for a strictly unbiased estimate of variance. The covariance of two variables x_i and x_j in $\boldsymbol{x}$ is

$$\begin{aligned} \sigma_{ij} &= \mathrm{E}\left[(x_i - \mu_i)(x_j - \mu_j)\right] \\ &= \mathrm{E}\left[x_i x_j\right] - \mu_i \mu_j \end{aligned} \tag{5.47}$$

The covariance is an average measure of the similarity of variation between the variables x_i and x_j. When the variables are statistically independent, their covariance is zero. When the variables are correlated to some degree, the covariance takes some non-zero value, and it is often useful to normalize this value so that its absolute maximum is unity by defining the correlation coefficient between the variables x_i and x_j for all vectors $\boldsymbol{x}$ associated with this class,

$$\rho_{ij} = \frac{\sigma_{ij}}{\sigma_i \sigma_j} = \frac{\sum (x_i - \mu_i)(x_j - \mu_j)}{\sqrt{\sum (x_i - \mu_i)^2 \sum (x_j - \mu_j)^2}} \tag{5.48}$$

The sample covariance matrix is defined:

$$\begin{aligned} \mathbf{C} &= \mathrm{E}\left[(\boldsymbol{x} - \boldsymbol{\mu})(\boldsymbol{x} - \boldsymbol{\mu})^t\right] \\ &= \mathrm{E}\left[\boldsymbol{x}\boldsymbol{x}^t\right] - \boldsymbol{\mu}\boldsymbol{\mu}^t \end{aligned} \tag{5.49}$$

and we see this matrix is constructed as

$$\mathbf{C} = \begin{pmatrix} \sigma_{11} & \cdots & \sigma_{1n} \\ \vdots & \ddots & \vdots \\ \sigma_{n1} & \cdots & \sigma_{nn} \end{pmatrix} = \begin{pmatrix} \sigma_1^2 & \cdots & \rho_{1n}\sigma_1\sigma_n \\ \vdots & \ddots & \vdots \\ \rho_{n1}\sigma_n\sigma_1 & \cdots & \sigma_n^2 \end{pmatrix} \tag{5.50}$$

When all the variables are statistically independent there is zero correlation between any pair of variables, so that $\mathbf{C}$ becomes a diagonal matrix with $C_{ij} = 0$ for all $i \neq j$, and $C_{ii} = \sigma_i^2$. As described in the previous section, the covariance matrix defines the shape of the distribution of feature vectors. Loci of points of constant density are hyper-ellipsoids with the principal axes in the directions of the eigenvectors of the covariance matrix, and with the marginal variances of the distribution along these axes determined by the eigenvalues. The covariance matrix estimated from (5.49) is an $n \times n$ symmetric positive-semidefinite matrix, but we must ensure that it is positive-definite so that it is non-singular and the inverse $\mathbf{C}^{-1}$ exists. Singularity occurs when there is a linear relationship between two or more variables in the general feature vector, resulting in one or more zero eigenvalues of the covariance matrix. The distribution of vectors collapses into a hyperplane with zero variance in the direction perpendicular to the plane. This situation is not unlikely, especially when there are a relatively large number of dimensions, and a relatively small number of data points. In general it is essential to sample a sufficient quantity of data in order to ensure the covariance matrices are well-conditioned. Needless to say, the larger the sample of data, the closer the estimates to the population statistics.

If the distribution of feature vectors for a particular class is not normal, there are other closed-form density functions which can be used in the same way (Duda and Hart, 1973 p64). If a class can be approximated by a set of normal modes, then a clustering procedure, as described in the previous section, may be used to identify prototypical clusters for parameter estimation. If class ω_i is represented by k normal modes $\omega_{i1}, \ldots, \omega_{ik}$, then the likelihood of an observation x in class ω_i is

$$p(x/\omega_i) = \sum_{j=1}^{k} p(x/\omega_{ij}) \qquad (5.51)$$

Alternatively, class-conditional densities may be approximated by other methods, such as Parzen estimators (Parzen, 1962) or Gaussian mixtures (Robins, 1948).

Finally we discuss a probabilistic distance measure which is an alternative concept of class separability to the inter-class distance described in the previous section. This measure can be used as an objective function in a clustering procedure, and also as a performance index for assessing the efficacy of a selected feature set in terms of the discriminating power of a subsequent classifier.

The goal of feature selection and clustering is to achieve a minimum classification error probability, but it is not computationally feasible to use the average error probability as a practical measure of class separability. The inter-class distance described in the previous section provides a concept of class separability which is computationally attractive, but is only loosely related to the error probability, because it does not account for the local probability structure. Probabilistic measures offer a more realistic concept of class separability by describing the overlap between adjacent probability density functions. There are a number of probabilistic distance measures (Devijver and Kittler, 1982 p257), and one example is the Bhattacharyya distance,

$$J_{ij} = -\ln \int \left[\mathrm{p}(\boldsymbol{x}/\omega_i)\mathrm{p}(\boldsymbol{x}/\omega_j) \right]^{\frac{1}{2}} d\boldsymbol{x} \qquad (5.52)$$

which is a measure of the overlap between two likelihood functions which characterize the pattern classes ω_i and ω_j. When a normal distribution is assumed, the closed-form solution of this integral is (Devijver and Kittler, 1982 p260)

$$J_{ij} = \tfrac{1}{8}(\boldsymbol{\mu}_j - \boldsymbol{\mu}_i)^t \left[\frac{\mathbf{C}_j + \mathbf{C}_i}{2} \right]^{-1} (\boldsymbol{\mu}_j - \boldsymbol{\mu}_i) + \tfrac{1}{2}\ln \frac{|\tfrac{1}{2}(\mathbf{C}_j + \mathbf{C}_i)|}{(|\mathbf{C}_j||\mathbf{C}_i|)^{\frac{1}{2}}}$$
$$(5.53)$$

where the maximum likelihood estimates of mean $\boldsymbol{\mu}$ and covariance $\mathbf{C}$ for the distributions of sample vectors in the ith and jth clusters respectively are obtained from (5.45) and (5.49). The Bhattacharyya distance is closely related to the pointwise error probability, but is much easier to compute. It has a number of remarkable properties which make it a useful measure of expected performance in the sense of class separation. In particular, it is sensitive to the relative orientation of the respective distributions, it is scale invariant, and it is also independent of the dimensionality of the feature space. The Bhattacharyya distance can therefore be used as

149

the basis of a comparison between the performance of different feature sets. We note that there is no obvious way to generalize (5.53) for the m-class case, and so it is necessary to use an average pairwise distance, as for the inter-class distance (5.21).

5.3. Composite model

Following Chapter 2 we will consider speech patterns as a composite of structural and quantitative forms of information. The proposed model is a hybrid of knowledge-based and pattern-matching methods, and is essentially a stochastic state-transition model with discrete transition probabilities and continuous observation probabilities, but with embedded structure to define transition sequences, where the embedded structure is a representation of *a priori* linguistic and phonological knowledge. In Chapter 3 we argued the case for incorporating top-down structural knowledge into the sequential pattern recognition process as the only solution to the problem of inferring an adequate and parsimonious structural account of speech patterns. The use of a principled linguistic theory to define pattern structure in the model employs the constraints in speech and language to contain the search through state sequences. A principled theory will capture important generalizations of structure, and in addition will permit a focus of attention onto specialized details crucial to pattern discrimination. An important aspect of the proposed model is that the knowledge can be formulated in a lucid declarative form so that it remains comprehensible and can be easily maintained and modified. For this reason we have chosen a grammatical form for the knowledge, and in the following chapter we illustrate how useful speech knowledge can be written in this form.

The model is based upon a context-free grammar $G = (V_n, V_t, P, S)$ where V_n is a set of non-terminal symbols, V_t is a set of terminal symbols, P is a set of production rules, and S is the initial symbol. A production rule in P has the general form $[A_1]A[A_2] \to \alpha$, where $A \in V_n$ and $\alpha \in (V_n \cup$

$V_t)^*$, and A_1, $A_2 \in (V_n \cup V_t)$ are optional context dependency specifiers, as described in Chapter 2. Each terminal symbol $T_k \in V_t$ which, in Chapter 2, was associated with a universal set of duration measurements, is here associated with an n-dimensional feature space Ω_k.

The relationship between the grammatical description of pattern structure and the numerical representation of the primitive pattern components is represented declaratively by symbolic *qualifiers* attached to symbols in the grammar. For example, in the production rule

$$\text{abrupt\_onset} \rightarrow \text{stop}, (\text{steep})\text{onset}.$$

the category 'onset' is a terminal symbol with attached qualifier 'steep'. The qualifier is generally some adjective which qualifies a (vector) value associated with the symbol. A qualified terminal will be denoted generally by $(j)T_k$, where $T_k \in V_t$, and $j \in A_k$, an alphabet of symbolic qualifiers associated with T_k. The qualifier is also the name of a pattern class in the feature space associated with the symbol, and we will characterize this pattern class by estimating the parameters of the class-conditional probability density function. The procedural interpretation of a qualifier 'j' is a reference to a pattern class $\omega_j(k) \subseteq \Omega_k$, and in particular to a set of parameters for the class-conditional probability density function $p(\boldsymbol{x}/\omega_j)$. This function describes the likelihood that a pattern vector $\boldsymbol{x}$ is a member of the class $\omega_j(k)$. (Where there is no need to distinguish between particular terminal symbols, the argument k will be dropped for convenience).

The grammatical description of pattern structure is related to a numerical pattern representation through pattern-matching procedures operating at terminal symbols. (Later we will see pattern-matching at non-terminals). Unknown pattern vectors are assigned membership of a particular class of pattern primitive with a probability. The probability, essentially a "score", is used to condition the parsing process and identify unknown pattern sequences by maximum likelihood evidential reasoning, as will be described.

5.3.1. Sequential decisions

Consider first the case of non-sequential decisions. The problem is to decide which class ω_j, of a set of classes in the alphabet A_k, represents the true "state of nature", having observed a pattern vector x at a particular instant of time. The decision is based upon the *a posteriori* probability $P(\omega_j/x)$ which is the probability that ω_j is the true "state of nature", having observed a pattern vector x. The maximum *a posteriori* probability (MAP) decision rule (5.35) assigns an observation x to class ω_j according to the rule:

$$\text{assign } x \text{ to } \omega_j(k) \text{ if } \Pr(\omega_j/x) > \Pr(\omega_i/x) \text{ for all } i \neq j \in A_k$$
$$(5.54)$$

Applying Bayes theorem we have the equivalent MAP rule (5.38) in terms of the *a priori* probability and the likelihood. If normal density functions are assumed, then the logarithmic form of the rule, (5.41) and (5.43), may be applied.

This classification model is extended to consider the problem of N sequential dependent decisions. The problem can be seen in two ways (Devijver and Kittler, 1982): as a *compound decision problem* in which a joint decision is made after N observations, or as a *sequential compound decision problem* in which an optimal decision is made at each observation.

In general the sequential compound decision problem is complicated by the necessity to compute high-order conditional probabilities in both "forward" and "backward" directions from a particular decision point. This complexity can be reduced, as in the case of hidden Markov models (Baum, 1972), by restricting the range of the probabilistic dependence. In the model to be described, the compound decision approach is used to take advantage of the grammatical derivation of sequences of terminal symbols, but it will be shown how sequential decisions can be made by a justifiable weakening of the decision rule.

Let the set of all pattern classes be

$$W = \{\omega_j(k) \mid T_k \in V_t, j \in A_k\} \qquad (5.55)$$

Let the set of ordered N-tuples of pattern classes, the N-fold cartesian product of W, be denoted

$$W^N = \{w_1, \ldots, w_i, \ldots\} \qquad (5.56)$$

where $w_i \in W^N$ is a sequence of N classes. For a matrix of N observation vectors $X = (x_1, \ldots, x_N)$, the MAP rule (5.35) is extended to make the compound decision w_i conditioned upon the observation sequence X,

$$\begin{aligned} \text{assign } X \text{ to } w_i \text{ if } \Pr(w_i/X) &> \Pr(w_j/X) \\ \text{for all } w_j \neq w_i &\in W^N \end{aligned} \qquad (5.57)$$

We apply Bayes rule to derive the equivalent MAP decision rule (5.38) in terms of $\Pr(X/w_i)$, the likelihood for observation sequence X conditioned upon class sequence w_i, and $\Pr(w_i)$, the *a priori* probability for a class sequence w_i.

The evaluation of (5.57) is based upon the enumeration of all the N-tuple strings, and is clearly impractical unless W is trivially small. One proposed solution is to order the N-tuples in decreasing probability (Aho *et al*, 1980), however this is unnecessary if a set of grammar rules is used to generate a string language over W.

The language $L(G)$ generated by a grammar G specifies a set of strings

$$L(G) = \{v \mid v \in V_t^*, S \overset{*}{\Rightarrow} v\} \qquad (5.58)$$

Each terminal symbol $(j)T_k$ in a string $v_i \in L(G)$ is a reference to a pattern class $\omega_j(k)$, and so a string of terminals v_i corresponds to a sequence of classes w_i. The language can then be defined in terms of pattern-class sequences, so that $w_i \in L(G)$ if $v_i \in L(G)$, and each terminal symbol in v_i references a corresponding pattern class in w_i. For N observations, the compound decision rule is based upon the set of N-tuples of pattern classes which are also in the language, so that the decision rule considers only class sequences w_i in the set $W^N \cap L(G)$, which is generally a lot smaller than W^N. Following Bayes rule, as described, the rule (5.57) becomes

assign X to w_i if $\Pr(w_i)\Pr(X/w_i) > \Pr(w_j)\Pr(X/w_j)$
$$\text{for all } w_j \neq w_i \in W^N \cap L(G) \qquad (5.59)$$

The set $W^N \cap L(G)$ is enumerated, to evaluate the rule (5.59), by a parsing process which generates $L(G)$, and in particular strings $v_i \in L(G)$ of N symbols. The following two sections describe the evaluation of the likelihood $\Pr(X/w_i)$ and the *a priori* probability $\Pr(w_i)$ respectively.

5.3.2. Likelihood functions in sequence

In order to simplify the computation of $\Pr(X/w_i)$ it is assumed that each vector x_j in X is dependent only upon the corresponding class ω_j in w_i, so that the joint density is simply the product of the component densities

$$\Pr(X/w_i) = \prod_{j=1}^{N} p(x_j/\omega_j) \qquad (5.60)$$

where ω_j is the pattern class referenced by the jth symbol in the derived terminal string v_i. When a pattern class ω_j is multi-modal, with k modes $\omega_{j1}, \ldots, \omega_{jk}$, then the likelihood of an observation x in class ω_j is given by (5.51). We note that the logarithmic form of the decision rule (5.41) is more efficient in practice as the product (5.60) becomes a sum. The assumption of independence between successive observations is acceptable provided the classes themselves are not considered independent. Probabilistic dependence between sequential classes is considered in the next section.

5.3.3. Stochastic grammar: a priori probabilities in sequence

Stochastic grammar will be introduced as a means to incorporate the *a priori* sequence probabilities $\Pr(w_i)$ into a grammatical formulation.

In practical applications structural patterns may exhibit non-determinacy and ambiguity as a result of noise in the pattern measurements, segmentation errors, and errors in primitive feature extraction. Two noteworthy techniques, stochastic grammar and error-correcting parsing, are used to provide criteria for ordering these alternative syntactic derivations, so as to describe noisy and distorted structural patterns under ambiguous situations.

Error correcting parsers (Lu and Fu, 1977) are a practical though somewhat inefficient approach to the recognition of noisy patterns. During the parsing process the original grammar is expanded to include all possible error situations, according to the introduction of insertion, substitution, and deletion errors. The error correction is achieved by selecting derivations using a string-to-string distance measure, such as that proposed by Aho and Peterson (1972). The need to extend the parsing process to include all possible error situations is traded off against the error correcting capability, but is nevertheless a serious drawback for this technique.

Stochastic grammar (Fu, 1982) is a means to incorporate statistics into grammatical formulations. It will be described as a means of summarising the computation, and the estimation problem, of *a priori* sequence probabilities, $\Pr(w_i)$. If P

is a set of productions in a grammar G, then each rule $r \in P$ is assigned a probability measure $\Pr(r)$. In the derivation of a string v_i, in M steps, each an application of a rule r,

$$S \xrightarrow{r_1} \alpha_1 \xrightarrow{r_2} \alpha_2 \Longrightarrow \cdots \xrightarrow{r_M} \alpha_M = v_i \in V_t^* \qquad (5.61)$$

the probability of deriving string v_i is given by (5.29)

$$\Pr(v_i) = \prod_{j=1}^{M} \Pr(r_j / r_1 r_2 \ldots r_{j-1}) \qquad (5.62)$$

where $\Pr(r_j / r_1 r_2 \ldots r_{j-1})$ is the conditional probability associated with the production rule r_j given that rules r_1, r_2, to r_{j-1} have previously been applied.

The advantages of stochastic grammar for the representation of sequence probabilities are those of ordinary grammar for the representation of strings of symbols, being in particular that a large number of sequences can be represented by a relatively small grammar. Parsing methods for stochastic grammars are essentially the same as for ordinary grammars, except that probabilities are used as the criterion to resolve each non-deterministic decision. In order to simplify the computation of conditional probabilities, and the estimation of production probabilities, the productions will be assumed to be *unrestricted*, so that

$$\Pr(r_j / r_1 r_2 \ldots r_{j-1}) = \Pr(r_j) \qquad (5.63)$$

If a sequence of decisions w_i leads to the derivation of a string v_i, in M steps each being the application of a production rule r, then the *a priori* sequence probability is given by (5.27)

$$\Pr(w_i) = \prod_{j=1}^{M} \Pr(r_j) \qquad (5.64)$$

The *a priori* sequence probability is thus decomposed into component probabilities implemented at the rule level. Probabilistic dependence extends across all symbols on the right-hand-side of a rule, and is summarized for each rule r by the *a priori* probability assignment $\Pr(r)$. We note that the product (5.64) becomes a sum of log probabilities using the logarithmic decision rule (5.41).

The probability $\Pr(r)$ is essentially a state-transition probability, and we see the dependence extends beyond successive states to sequences of states, depending upon the form of the production rules in the grammar. Of course if the grammar contains no centre-embedded productions, and we limit the depth of recursion, then it can be translated into *regular* form with productions $A \rightarrow aB$, where $A, B \in V_n$ and $a \in V_t$. In this case the state transition probability is Markovian. However, estimation of the rule probabilities with *context-free* rules captures the statistics of important structural generalities. It is interesting to note that a hidden Markov model (HMM) based upon continuous probability density functions can be formulated in terms of the hybrid model described. State transitions in the HMM are equivalent to regular grammar rules of the general form

$$q_1 \xrightarrow{a_{12}} (b_2)q_2$$

This rule describes a transition between states q_1 and q_2 with probability $\Pr(a_{12})$, which is equivalent to one element of the HMM $\mathbf{A}$ matrix (3.23). The qualifier b_2 references a likelihood function $p(x/b_2)$ for observations x in class b_2 given state q_2, and this is equivalent to the $\mathbf{B}$ vector of likelihood functions in a continuous HMM ((3.22) *et seq*).

Clearly a lot of rules are required for even a low-order HMM, but this is because the HMM must provide for all possible sequences. This illustrates the advantages of parsimony or representational economy in the use of context-free rules.

5.3.4. Parameter estimation

We will assume that the pattern vectors are normally distributed in an n-dimensional feature space, so the class-conditional likelihood function is the multivariate normal density function (5.40) $N(\mu_j, C_j)$, where the parameters are the mean vector μ_j and the covariance matrix C_j of the jth pattern class. A multi-modal class is parameterized by a set of mean vectors $\mu_{j1}, \ldots, \mu_{jk}$, and a set of covariance matrices $C_{j1}, \ldots, C_{jk}$. Parameter estimation in the probabilistic case is simply the computation of appropriate summary statistics of the cluster of pattern vectors representative of a particular pattern class. The maximum likelihood estimates of mean μ and covariance C, for a cluster of N sample vectors x_i, are respectively given by (5.45) and (5.49).

The parameter estimation procedure is a *supervized* approach (Devijver and Kittler, 1982) in which mean and covariance is estimated from a set of pattern vectors known to belong to a particular class. The process is complicated by the fact that the distribution of pattern vectors may not be normal, and may even exhibit a number of *modes*, or distinct clusters, in the feature space. It will be assumed that all the modes are normal. It is necessary to characterize the distributions of pattern vectors so as to maximally separate the pattern classes in the feature space, where each class may be represented by one or more mode clusters. For each feature space Ω_k, pattern vectors $x \in \omega_j(k)$ are collected for all $j \in A_k$. A cluster analysis procedure then identifies clusters of pattern vectors representative of each class $\omega_j(k)$, with the objective of maximally separating classes $\omega_j(k)$ and $\omega_i(k)$ for all $i \neq j \in A_k$.

Prior to clustering, the population of all training vectors irrespective of class is scaled using the transformation (see section 5.2.2)

$$x' = \mathbf{W}^{-1}(x - \mu) \qquad (5.65)$$

where $\mathbf{W}$ is the diagonal matrix of the population standard deviations for each variable in x, and μ is the population mean vector. This transformation makes the variables in x independent of their original scales of measurement, from the viewpoint of cluster analysis, as the population of training vectors in the normalized space has zero mean and unit standard deviation along each coordinate axis of the n-dimensional feature space.

Cluster analysis aims to find k clusters in the feature space with $k \geq m$, where $m = |A_j|$ classes, so that each class may be represented by one or more normal modes. We use the K-means algorithm described in Section 5.2.2. The objective of the clustering procedure is to minimize the pointwise intra-class distance over all classes (the trace of matrix $\mathbf{S}_w$ (5.20)), given by

$$D_w = \frac{1}{k} \sum_{i=1}^{k} \sum_{j=1}^{K_i} \|x_j^{(i)} - \mu_i\|^2 \qquad (5.66)$$

where K_i is the number of points $x_j^{(i)}$ assigned to the the ith cluster. The results of a cluster analysis are assessed using a quality measure D_b/D_w, where D_b is the average pairwise inter-cluster distance for clusters of different classes (the trace of matrix $\mathbf{S}_b$ (5.21b)), given by

$$D_b = \frac{2}{m(m-1)} \sum_{i=1}^{k-1} \sum_{j=i+1}^{k} J_{ij} \quad , \quad \omega_i \neq \omega_j \qquad (5.67)$$

The inter-cluster distance may be defined $J_{ij} = \|\mu_i - \mu_j\|^2$, as for (5.21b), or using a probabilistic distance such as the

159

Bhattacharyya distance (5.53). This distance gives a more realistic picture of class separability, but requires the computation of the cluster covariance matrices. Having identified the modes of each pattern class, the parameters μ and C of each likelihood function can be estimated using (5.45) and (5.49).

Finally we need to estimate the production rule probabilities, for a given grammar, from a set of training observations. A re-estimation technique (Lee and Fu, 1972) uses the relative frequency of rule applications with respect to the set of rules which have the same non-terminal symbol on the left-hand-side. Let the number of times a production rule $A_i \rightarrow \alpha_j$ is used in the parsing of a terminal string be N_{ij}. Then the probability associated with production $A_i \rightarrow \alpha_j$ is the relative frequency of its occurrence with respect to all productions $A_i \rightarrow \alpha_k$ in G, where A_i is a particular non-terminal symbol, and $\alpha_k \in (V_t \cup V_n)^*$,

$$\hat{p}_{ij} = \frac{N_{ij}}{N_{ik}} \tag{5.68}$$

This estimate improves with each iteration for all terminal strings.

It should be pointed out that rule probabilities estimated in this way do not guarantee that the grammar is *consistent*, in the sense that

$$\sum_{v_i \in L(G)} P(v_i) = 1 \tag{5.69}$$

However such consistency again plays no part in the decision process, and so this is not considered a requirement. It is necessary only that the training set is representative of the population. Lee and Fu (1972) have proposed a variant of this re-estimation procedure which takes account of word-frequency in the training set and disproportionate ambiguity in the grammar.

5.4. The advantages of a "weak" decision rule

The decision rule (5.59) can be weakened in the sense introduced in Chapter 2, so that decisions are based upon a max-min rule rather than upon probability products, and this leads to a method for optimal sequential decisions, rather than purely compound decisions.

The prerequisite for the "weak" rule is that the likelihoods are a mapping $\mathcal{X}: x \to [0, 1]$, and that the functions have the properties of fuzzy relations, with regard to the combination of degrees of belief. The required properties for an *admissible* fuzzy set (Zadeh, 1975) are:

1. $0 \leq \mathcal{X}(\boldsymbol{x}) \leq 1$ for all $\boldsymbol{x}$.
2. $\mathcal{X}$ is a transitive relation on the set of all vectors in the space Ω. That is:

$$\text{if } \mathcal{X}(\boldsymbol{x}_1) > \mathcal{X}(\boldsymbol{x}_2) \text{ and } \mathcal{X}(\boldsymbol{x}_2) > \mathcal{X}(\boldsymbol{x}_3)$$
$$\text{then } \mathcal{X}(\boldsymbol{x}_1) > \mathcal{X}(\boldsymbol{x}_3)$$

These conditions can be met by simply leaving off the normalization factor in the definition of the continuous normal probability density function (5.40), so that the fuzzy-set membership function [6] of class ω_j is:

$$\mathcal{X}_{\omega_{ij}}(\boldsymbol{x}) = \exp\left[-\tfrac{1}{2}(\boldsymbol{x} - \boldsymbol{\mu}_{ij})^t C_{ij}^{-1}(\boldsymbol{x} - \boldsymbol{\mu}_{ij})\right] \qquad (5.70)$$

---

[6] The use of multivariate fuzzy-set membership functions to classify speech features is reported by Pal and Majumdar (1977). The approach described here differs from theirs in the use of the covariance matrix to provide feature weighting.

where the parameters are estimated for the jth mode in the ith class. The normalization factor which has been dropped serves only to ensure the density function has unit volume. It should however be noted that scaling density functions to unit maximum in this way does shift the decision boundary between classes. This is not a problem provided the classes are reasonably well separated, or have similar variances, and that the variances are not excessively large.

The equivalent form of the MAP decision rule (5.57) using fuzzy-set membership functions maximizes $\text{bel}(w_i/X)$, the *degree of belief* in the sequence of classes w_i, given observation sequence X. By analogy with (5.38), a "weak" rule equivalent to (5.59) is

$$\text{assign } X \text{ to } w_i \text{ if}$$

$$\text{bel}(w_i) \bigwedge \text{bel}(X/w_i) > \text{bel}(w_j) \bigwedge \text{bel}(X/w_j) \qquad (5.71)$$

$$\text{for all } w_j \neq w_i \in W^N \cap L(G)$$

where $\wedge$ is the *min* operator. The product of the *a priori* probability and likelihood (5.59) is here the logical intersection of two fuzzy sets (see section 2.4.3). The corresponding form of the likelihoods (5.60) and (5.51) is

$$\text{bel}(X/w_i) = \min_j \mathcal{X}_{\omega_j}(x_j) \qquad (5.72)$$

$$j = 1, \ldots, N \text{ observations.}$$

$$\mathcal{X}_{\omega_i}(x) = \max_j \mathcal{X}_{\omega_{ij}}(x) \qquad (5.73)$$

$$j = 1, \ldots, K \text{ modes for class } \omega_i.$$

and the corresponding form of the *a priori* sequence probabilities (5.64) is

$$\text{bel}(w_i) = \min_k \Pr(r_k) \qquad (5.74)$$

$k = 1, \ldots, M$ steps in the derivation of w_i

One obvious advantage of the weak rule and fuzzy-set membership functions is the elimination of the scaling problem. Computation of (5.59) will generally cause arithmetic underflow unless special precautions are taken to progressively scale the products.

Another advantage is that using the weak rule an admissible solution to (5.71) can be obtained without having to exhaustively parse all ambiguous derivations. This was shown in Chapter 2 (2.21), and the equivalent statement which follows from (5.72) and (5.74) is

$$\text{bel}(w_i/\boldsymbol{X}) < \text{bel}(w_j/\boldsymbol{X}) \qquad (5.75)$$

if there exists $1 \leq k \leq N_i$ such that

$$\chi_{\omega_k}(\boldsymbol{x}_k) < \text{bel}(w_j/\boldsymbol{X})$$

or if there exists $1 \leq k \leq M_i$ such that

$$\text{P}(r_k) < \text{bel}(w_j/\boldsymbol{X})$$

A derivation therefore fails as soon as the local evidence grade falls below the current maximum. In this way optimal local sequential decisions can be made by what is essentially a *branch and bound* decision process (Winston, 1984). Rule probabilities are tested using the condition (5.75) upon application of a rule, so that less likely rules are not applied until the more likely rules have already failed.

The decision rules (5.59) and (5.71) obtain an optimal compound decision. The condition (5.75) enables optimal decisions to be taken sequentially, by maintaining a prescribed number of the better decision sequences in parallel. The procedure for sequential decisions is based on a *priority ordering* of the N "best" derivations from a non-terminal symbol, in the sense of greatest degree of belief. Assuming a top-down left-to-right parsing algorithm, at each non-terminal symbol generate and record the N best derivations, or record failure if none can be found. The number N can be specified for individual non-terminals by a grammatical annotation, and functions as a variable width "search beam". The recorded derivations include all attributed information, and the derivations are recorded such that subsequent access is ordered according to the composite evidence grade. Thus the highest priority recorded derivations are considered first. These partial results are available to the parsing process so that unnecessary duplication of effort may be avoided. In addition, the search is "pruned" by rejecting poorly graded derivations as early as possible in the search for the N best.

The pruning of poorly graded decision sequences is based upon a *cut point* or threshold. Let the cut point $\lambda \in [0,1]$ of the language, in terms of the max-min composition of evidence grades, define a language:

$$ L(G, \lambda) = \{v_i \mid v_i \in V_t^*, S \overset{*}{\Rightarrow} v_i, \mathrm{bel}(w_i/\boldsymbol{X}) > \lambda\} \qquad (5.76) $$

where w_i is the sequence of classes and $\boldsymbol{X}$ the sequence of pattern vectors corresponding to the terminal string v_i. From (5.75) it follows that a necessary condition for local evidence grade is $\chi_\omega(\boldsymbol{x}) > \lambda$ The cut-point is thus a threshold below which all evidence is considered insufficient, and all such lines of reasoning are pruned. The method for evaluating the N best derivations from an annotated non-terminal is summarized in the algorithm given in Figure 5.2. Essentially, the procedure is to evaluate N derivations from a non-terminal, and then set the cut-point equal to the lowest composite evidence grade of the N derivations. Any subsequent derivation

1. Parse the first N derivations from non-terminal 'A'.

   1.1 If no successful derivations, record failure.

   1.2 If less than N successful derivations, record them.

   1.3 If N successful derivations, order them and search for more as follows:

2. Push poorest composite evidence grade of N derivations onto cut-point stack.

   2.1 Parse one next derivation. If fail, exit to 3.

   2.2 Delete the poorest of N derivations and insert the new derivation.

   2.3 Replace head of cut-point stack with new poorest composite evidence grade.

   2.4 Repeat 2.1 and sequence.

3. Pop head of cut-point stack.

4. Record N best successful derivations.

Figure 5.2. Priority ordering of derivations

from this non-terminal is abandoned as soon as any component of evidence falls below the current cut-point, because (5.75) guarantees that the eventual result of this derivation cannot be any better than the poorest of the N derivations so far accumulated. Under these conditions any successful derivation must be better than the poorest of the N derivations, and can be swapped into the accumulating list of best derivations.

The cut-point is maintained on a globally accessible cut-point stack. The initial head of this stack is the cut point of the language, λ. Local cut-points are pushed onto the stack following N derivations from an annotated non-terminal, so that the scope of the current cut-point, at the head of the stack, applies to the appropriate derivation. Embedded recursive calls to annotated non-terminals have a corresponding local scope. Following (5.75), the cut-point stack is guaranteed to be ordered, with lower values nearer the head.

A final advantage of the weak rule is that decisions are independent of the length of the observation sequence. It is then meaningful to compare sequences of different lengths using the max-min rule, where it is not meaningful to do so for products of probabilities. It is possible therefore to consider additional "hidden" observations at non-terminal symbols.

The model is extended so that every symbol may be associated with a feature space. In order to relate the hidden observations to observations at the terminal level, each production rule $A \rightarrow \alpha$, where $A \in V_n$ and $\alpha \in (V_n \cup V_t)^*$, is associated with a function $f_r \colon X_\alpha \rightarrow x_A$, where x_A is a feature vector in the space associated with non-terminal symbol A, and X_α is the concatenation of feature vectors associated with the members of α. The function f_r defines a vector subspace associated with the category A in terms of the vector spaces associated with α. The only restriction upon f_r is that it treats categories consistently. That is, the function f_r maps onto the same sub-space for each rule with category A on the left-hand side. Using mapping functions to relate observations provides a means to refine and compress measurement data by projecting it onto a lower sub-space in which the pattern classes are maximally separated. The mapping functions propagate quantitative information throughout the syntactic process, and offer a very flexible method for decomposing the pattern information into sequential classes subject to contextual constraints.

5.5. Summary

The hybrid model for composite pattern recognition, described in section 5.3, is based upon a stochastic context-free grammar, with probabilistic pattern-matching at the terminal level. The model is defined by three parameter sets.

1. A given grammar, which is a formulation of linguistic knowledge.
2. The parameters of the likelihood functions (5.40), which are estimated from labelled training data (5.45) (5.49).
3. The set of production rule probabilities, which are incrementally re-estimated using the relative frequency of rule application during training, (5.68).

The decision rule (5.59) classifies an unknown sequence of observations by selecting one derivation from a number of ambiguous derivations on the basis of maximum *a posteriori* probability. The calculation of *a posteriori* probability uses the likelihood functions, (5.60) and (5.51), and the sequence probabilities, in terms of rule probabilities for stochastic grammar (5.64). The equivalent logarithmic form of the decision rule, (5.41) and (5.43), is computationally more efficient in practice. A "weak" decision rule (5.71) based on the max-min composition of evidence grades enables optimal sequential decisions between class sequences of different length, so that numerical pattern-matching may be an integral part of the syntactic structure, at both terminals and non-terminals.

CHAPTER 6

Modelling allophonic and phonotactic constraints

6.1. Introduction

A specific model will be developed on the basis of the general hybrid model described in the last chapter, Sections 5.3 and 5.4. The specific model proposed in this chapter serves a dual purpose. Firstly, it illustrates a well-motivated approach to the formulation of pattern grammars in the application of speech knowledge to a practical and real recognition problem. Secondly, it generates information on the strength and generality of certain contrasts in terms of the selected features.

The specific model is designed to classify certain intermediate linguistic units, between the acoustic signal and whole words. This is the approach advocated by Zue and his colleagues (Shipman and Zue, 1982; Huttenlocher and Zue, 1984) whose work seems to indicate that a detailed phonetic transcription may not be an essential goal for the early stages of a speech recognition system. The intermediate units represent a partial refinement of the signal representation which is capable of significantly reducing large lexical search spaces.

Instead of the detailed serial pattern-matching search of a large lexicon, Zue suggests that broad categories are used to access a relatively small subset of the lexicon, and reject the majority of words which are immediately incompatible with the partial representation. Given a small subset of words, the problem of verification using more detailed pattern information is greatly simplified.

In large-vocabulary experiments, Zue and colleagues have shown that a partial phonetic transcription into only six broad categories: stop, strong fricative, weak fricative, nasal, liquid/glide, and vowel, is capable of identifying a subset of candidate words, with a mean size of two words, from a vocabulary of 20,000 words. Pisoni (1985) has also reported significant reductions in the search space, using still broader classes such as the number of phonemes in a word, and vowel/consonant classification. Despite the coarse level of phonetic description, a dramatic reduction in the lexical search space is obtained for subsequent detailed matching.

In the experiments mentioned above, the transcription used is a partial phonetic transcription of every phoneme. Consequently any insertion, substitution, or deletion errors which are manifest at the level of this broad transcription will result in erroneous lexical access, which may be extremely difficult to recover from. For example words such as 'factory' and 'boundary' are susceptible to deletion of the middle syllable. Words such as 'bubbling' and 'wrestling' are often articulated with three syllables. Broad substitutions are common, particularly at word boundaries, for instance 'did # you', in which the juncture may easily come to resemble a voiced fricative.

In order to contain the complexity of lexical access using partial phonetic information it is necessary also to delimit the words in the string of phonetic units. This requires the extraction of word boundary or syllabification cues.

The errors which result in an imperfect partial transcription can be corrected by multiple lexical entries, or by error-correcting rules based upon phonological constraints at the level of the broad transcription or in a second resyllabification pass. However this defeats the object by generating additional complexity. What is required is a strategy for lexical access based upon imperfect partial transcriptions, and partial syllabification information, which would incorporate some means of applying knowledge concerning the degree of expected variance associated with individual transcribed units. The problem will not be further considered. The proposed model is designed to transcribe broadly the acoustic signal based upon what is in the signal, and not upon what ought to be in the signal. This is a significant simplification of the problem so that the applied knowledge may be usefully restricted to the domains of phonotactics and allophonic variation.

The constraint domains of phonotactics and allophonic variants are generalized at the level of the syllable, and embodied within a grammatical structure of linguistic constituents. The syllable structure defines the context for particular acoustic realizations of phonetic units, and in turn the classification of particular phonetic units can be said to provide cues to syllabification.

6.2. Phonotactic and allophonic knowledge

The pattern constraints contained in the hybrid model take the form of structural constraints in the domain of phonotactics, and quantitative constraints in the domain of allophonic variants. The structural constraints are represented by a complete grammatical description of the set of phonotactically correct sequences of phonetic units; a language which has the syllable as its root category. Allophonic variants are represented by symbolic qualifiers ('short', 'long', etc.) as described in Chapter 5. These qualifiers reference probabilistic likelihood functions which describe the quantitative characteristics of each allophonic variant.

6.2.1. Phonotactic constraints

Phonotactic constraints concern the order of phonetic units. They derive in part from physiological constraints, but mainly from the phonology of the language. The set of phonotactic constraints associated with one language will be different from those associated with another. The extent to which phonotactic constraints are also dialect-dependent is a matter of debate, but the phonotactics of a given dialect are speaker-independent.

The phonotactic constraints which are applied here relate to the *received pronunciation* of British English as described by Gimson (p237 *et seq* 1984). Gimson provides a comprehensive specification of phonotactically correct sequences of constituents at the syllabic level.

An immediate advantage which can be seen in these constraints is the very limited length and complexity of consonant clusters. This significantly reduces the amount of grammatical description required. The model describes clusters to a complexity of three consonants before a vowel (CCCV), and two following a vowel (VCC), as for example in "**stretched strap**". The sequence constraints also provide cues to syllabification since syllabic structure is defined in terms of phonotactically correct sequences. For example, the following syllabic junctures are unambiguously defined by phonotactic constraints:

'**red#imp**'   -because the short vowel in '**red**' must be followed by a syllabic coda.

'**red#stamp**' -because the voiced stop in coda position may not precede a voiceless consonant in a cluster.

'**#hang#**'   -because /h/ is always in syllable onset position, and /ng/ is always in coda position.

6.2.2. Allophonic constraints

Allophonic variants are context-dependent acoustic realizations of phonetic units. The allophonic variants of a phoneme are produced as a result of coarticulation, and consequently are classified subject to context. Allophonic rules (Ladefoged, 1982) are context-sensitive re-write rules which map a general description of a phonetic unit, in terms of distinctive features [1], onto a special one.

Allophonic rules are by nature generative rules, and from a recognition point of view their application as context-sensitive re-write rules produces more complexity than it resolves. Thus it was believed that allophonic variants contribute nothing but noise to the speech signal. However allophonic rules can be re-formulated so as to exploit the information which is implicit in the positioning of a particular variant with respect to its local context.

The context-sensitive re-write rules for allophones can be re-formulated as context-free rules, where the context associated with a particular variant is incorporated within the immediate generalization of the local sequence of units as a constituent of a syllable. Church (1983) has pointed out that this can be done so as to take advantage of the fact that many general types of effect occur in similar contexts. When these contexts are associated with particular constituents of a syllable, (for example 'onset', 'coda', etc), then the general variant effects can be isolated from one another, and their underlying characteristics can be specialized.

For example, the context dependency #_V (ie. something which depends upon the following vowel) is implicit in a new category 'onset', where 'onset' is constrained to precede 'peak' as a constituent of a syllable. Thus the general variant effect described by the allophonic rule:

$$\begin{bmatrix} -\texttt{voiced} \\ +\texttt{stop} \end{bmatrix} \rightarrow [+\texttt{aspirated}] \quad \text{when syllable initial}$$

---

[1]   The term *distinctive feature* refers to a component of a specific system of phonological description (Jakobson, Fant and Halle, 1961; Chomsky and Halle, 1968), and is related to but distinct from the more general usage of the term *feature* as a measurement in the pattern recognition sense.

is restricted to syllabic onset position in the following fragment of context-free grammar:

```
syllable  →  syl_onset, rhyme.
syl_onset  →  uv_stop.
uv_stop  →  (short_strong)fric, onset.
```

Having isolated the unvoiced stop in syllable initial position, a variant is described by a specific qualifier 'short_strong', which characterizes the duration and intensity of this aspiration measurement in the feature space associated with the category 'fric'. This specialization results in a less-variant classification of particular allophones, in a given position with respect to the syllable. Therefore allophonic variants can be said to contribute information, rather than just noise.

Allophonic variants contribute cues to syllabification which are implicit in their position with respect to the syllable. For example the allophone of the unvoiced fricative /s/ in syllable initial position has significantly stronger frication than the corresponding allophone in syllable final position. The specialized classification of such allophones can therefore be used to resolve syllabification decisions such as 'pea stalks'/'peace talks'.

The inventory of required allophonic variants is both language and dialect dependent. Certain variants are relatively speaker independent, others less so. The acoustic invariance of allophones is a subject of great debate (Stevens and Blumstein, 1981; Lisker, 1985). Although certain variants can be automatically classified with high reliability across a range of speakers (for example strong initial frication), the nature of speaker dependent variations is complex and difficult to formulate. Rather than view this as a problem of insufficient rules or features, it is perhaps better considered as a function of speaker adaptation. However, the method by which a composite pattern recognizer can adapt on-the-fly to a "style" of pattern, and the information which cues this process, is an extremely difficult topic. Lasry and Stern (1984) describe an interesting model for speaker adaptation based upon a statistical dependence between the mean vectors characteristic of allophonic variants, and propose a parameter estimation technique for the likelihood functions of this dependence. The recognizer proposed here will not take such dependence into consideration, and simply generates information on the strength and generality of allophonic classes, in terms of class separation, in order to test the adequacy of speculative pattern structure and primitive features.

6.3. Categorization

The choice of speech categories at every hierarchical level within the structural model is particularly important in order to optimize discrimination and to contain the combinatorics of the search. Categories are chosen to facilitate the linguistic performance of the grammar, and to exploit all available structural and quantitative constraints.

6.3.1. Terminal categories

Two factors motivate the choice of categories and their associated feature spaces at the terminal level. Firstly, the categories must be a specialization of syllabic constituents. If the categories comply with a general theory of linguistic constituents, then general linguistic constraints can be an inherent structural component of the model. Linguistic constituents are by nature a principled sub-division of significant and "interesting" higher-level categories, and the division process reflects the properties of the local constraint domain. For example, because many allophonic and phonological processes share the same environment, generalized variant effects can be captured by new categories, which embody the context dependency by their very position in a sequence of constituents. In addition, the structural constraints embody an element of expectation which can be used, for example, to guide the extraction of more subtle events. The spectrogram reader's strategy may be very broadly interpreted as follows: look for the most prominent events first, then use these events, plus a knowledge of what to expect, to search for more subtle events. This is a plausible explanation for the deceptively simple way a trained spectrogram reader can discriminate phonetic events, based upon very small-scale evidence such as the rising F_1 associated with syllable initial consonants, voice onset times, and so forth. Following this paradigm, feature extraction is guided by an expectation strategy which is encoded within the structural model, and which uses prominent speech events to guide the search for more subtle events. The main advantage of this paradigm is to contain the combinatorial explosion of classification possibilities, and also to order the feature extraction processes, with respect to the structural model. Terminal categories are then the most prominent events which also comply with the linguistic model. However, emphasis on prominent events must always be tempered by the difficulty of error recovery.

Secondly, the categories must exhibit a worthwhile degree of invariance, both for single speakers and across a range of speakers. Categories are selected such that the variation amongst corresponding measurement vectors sampled from the training data is contained by the respective classifiers without loss of discrimination. The performance index for the quality of class separation, described in the last chapter, can be used as an objective in this selection. Categories at which there is too much variation require explicit specialization into context-dependent sub-categories which are probabilistically distinct. This approach depends upon the existence of invariant categories, the use of which is likely to minimize the structural variation which remains to be explicitly represented. Following Stevens and Blumstein (1981), in order to perceive a segment as a particular category the signal must contain a degree of invariant primary information. A speaker must hit, or come sufficiently close to, certain target articulatory configurations in order to be intelligible. These targets are described by the domains of manner and place of articulation, and in turn by combinations of acoustic correlates. The secondary information, the joining material between targets, is also important for the correct identification of primary targets. Having observed the fact that in any particular feature space, with measurements made at a particular scale or resolution, some categories are more invariantly distinct or prominent than others, the conclusion is that no one space and scale is best for all categories. Primary sources of speech information occur over a wide range of feature spaces and observation scales, and classification of such information may require category-specific feature extraction. In the hybrid classifier described in the last chapter, each grammatical symbol may be associated with a category-specific feature space. Features may be extracted when required at the particular scale and space for which the target category is maximally distinct. Terminal categories represent the lowest level of this process, and the first refinement of the acoustic signal.

The terminal categories used here correspond to the elementary segments generated by the procedures described in Chapter 4. A terminal string is essentially a sequence of pattern vectors of feature measurements which describe the elementary segments. Each vector is labelled with a terminal symbol in order to distinguish the specific feature space in which measurements are made. Figure 6.1 lists the alphabet of terminal symbols, the corresponding measurement vectors, and the qualifier alphabet associated with each feature space. The examples given in the figure relate the terminal symbols to segment types. The measurements which characterize each segment type are as follows. For 'peak' and 'dip' the segment duration is measured in milliseconds, and the height measure, or segment intensity, is the mean height of the segment. For 'fric' (ie fricative) and 'burst' events, which consist of a high frequency onset, peak, and offset segments, the duration is measured from the beginning of the onset to the end of the offset. The height of intensity is measured as the mean height of the peak segment. The categories 'nfoot' and 'pfoot' are respectively a negative sloped segment between an 'offset' and a 'dip', and a positive sloped seg-

Terminal symbol	Measurement vector	Qualifier alphabet
a. peak	[duration,height]	{short,med,long, extralong}
b. dip	[duration,height]	{short_low,med_low, long_low,med_high}
c. onset	[slope]	{med,steep}
d. offset	[slope]	{med,steep}
e. pfoot	[length]	{short,long}
f. nfoot	[length]	{short,med,long}
g. fric	[duration,height]	{weak_burst, strong_burst, weak_fric,med_fric, strong_fric}

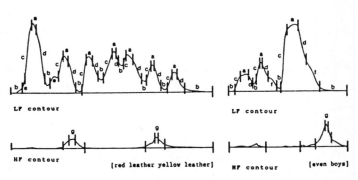

Figure 6.1. Terminal categories

ment between a 'dip' and an 'onset'. The length measure
for 'nfoot' and 'pfoot' is the distance along a straight line
between the segment bounds. The slopes of 'onset' and
'offset' segments are simply the vertical displacement of
the segment divided by the duration.

Although the features are rudimentary, the constraints
upon pattern structure are sufficient to refine the terminal
string into a surprisingly detailed string of manner of articulation classes.

177

The strings of pattern primitives are derived from the low and high frequency bandlimited energy contours described in Chapter 4. Following segmentation, the two strings are merged onto a single string by inserting high frequency events into the low frequency segment string, reducing the duration of unvoiced segments appropriately. The primitive string is labelled from the alphabet in Figure 6.1 using a simple deterministic process, and appropriate features are extracted.

6.3.2. Non-terminal categories

The intermediate categories in a context-free notation are chosen to capture significant linguistic generalizations, and consequently reduce the size of the grammar and the complexity of the search. Such categories represent general classes of phonetic event, in terms of the selected features. These general classes are then subject to general constraints. The non-terminal categories are syllabic constituents chosen to exploit these general constraints.

The hierarchies of non-terminal categories for syllable initial and syllable final consonants are shown in Figure 6.2. Figure 6.3 explains the non-terminal symbols and defines the phonotactically correct consonant clusters in terms of manner of articulation classes. The phonotactically correct sequences shown in Figure 6.3b and Figure 6.3c have been derived from tables of phonotactic possibilities (Gimson *et seq*, 1984 p237), generalized into broader manner of articulation categories. A certain amount of phonotactic detail is lost as a result of this process. For example, the statement that a syllable initial consonant cluster begins with a voiced stop, followed by a liquid or glide (`d.cluster`), disregards the constraint that /d/ cannot be followed by /l/, in favour of the otherwise strong generality of the statement. We cannot distinguish between liquids and glides in terms of the simple features used, and it is convenient to consider liquids and glides as a single category, (`lg`).

The principal non-terminal categories used in the model are 'onset' and 'coda' which are 'voiced/unvoiced' and

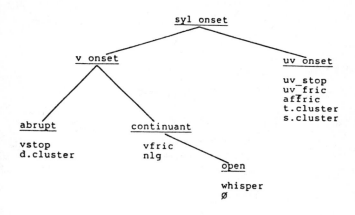

a

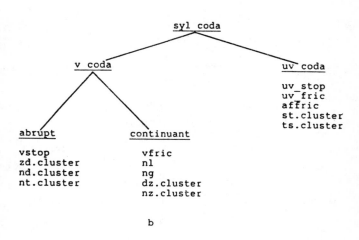

b

Figure 6.2. Non-terminal categories
(a) onset of syllable (b) coda of syllable

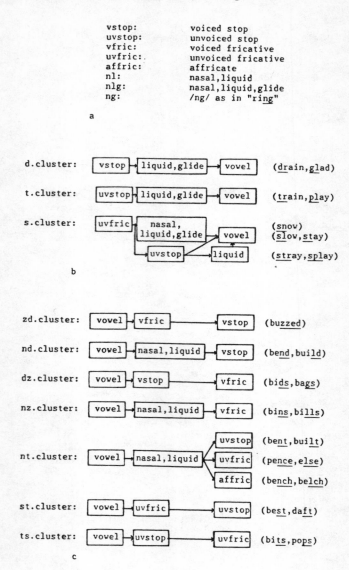

Figure 6.3. Non-terminal categories
(a) explanation of symbols
(b) syllable onset consonant clusters to CCCV
(c) syllable coda consonant clusters to VCC

'continuant/abrupt'. The voiced/unvoiced contrast is associated with the general quantitative effect of duration lengthening or shortening the immediately preceding constituent. General categories such as 'voiced_coda' are referred to by name in the specification of a context dependency, as described in Chapter 2, which implements the shortening/lengthening agreement between vowels and post-vocalic consonants. The continuant/abrupt contrast provides for general structural agreement across syllabic junctures. Continuant consonants are "semi-sonorant", and the category includes all consonants for which the evolution of low-frequency energy is continuous and not sharply interrupted. The abrupt consonants are those for which the low-frequency energy is abruptly curtailed by a complete closure at the lips or at the glottis.

In consonant clusters, the general voiced/unvoiced contrast refers to the first consonant in the cluster, so that a context dependency may be established between the specification of the cluster as a whole and the immediately preceding constituent. The general continuant/abrupt contrast refers to the last consonant in the cluster in order to relate the cluster to the immediately following constituent.

Figure 6.4 lists the manner of articulation categories which are identified by the grammar for inclusion in the parse list constructed during the recognition process. Strings of such categories constitute the partial phonetic transcription generated by the syllabic model.

6.4. The syllabic model

The complete grammar, listed in Appendix 1, is now described. Training results for model estimation are interspersed with the description of the grammar in order to illustrate the interdependence of contextual constraints, feature selection, and pattern-class separation.

The results are plots of the estimated likelihood functions (5.40) based upon a corpus of training data (see Appendix 2). Each plot reports the class mean (labelled M_i),

```
Peak.                Explanation.
short_vowel
long_vowel

Onset.

whisper
vstop               voiced stop
uvstop              unvoiced stop
vfric               voiced fricative
uvfric              unvoiced fricative
affric              affricate
nlg                 nasal, liquid, glide
lg                  liquid, glide
liquid

Coda.

vstop               voiced stop
uvstop              unvoiced stop
vfric               voiced fricative
uvfric              unvoiced fricative
affric              affricate
nl                  nasal, liquid
ng                  /ng/ phoneme
```

Figure 6.4. Broad manner-of-articulation classes

and the inter-class separation in terms of the Bhattacharyya distance (5.53) (labelled Jb_{ij}). Two-dimensional Gaussians are represented by pairs of concentric ellipses at one and two standard deviates from the mean respectively. All the plots show Gaussian density functions normalized to unit maximum to illustrate the decision boundaries using the max-min rule (5.71).

The grammar describes a sequence of syllables, optionally separated by a pause.

$$\text{phrase} \;\rightarrow\; \text{syl, pause, phrase.} \qquad (6.1)$$
$$\text{phrase} \;\rightarrow\; \emptyset. \qquad (6.2)$$

$$\text{pause} \;\rightarrow\; \text{(long\_low)dip.} \qquad (6.3)$$
$$\text{pause} \;\rightarrow\; \emptyset. \qquad (6.4)$$

The syllable is immediately sub-divided into an onset phase and a rhyme phase. The importance of the rhyme is as a generalization of the phonotactic variation between syllabic peak and the coda; a short or "lax" vowel must be followed by a coda (at least one consonant), although a long or "tense" vowel may be an open syllable.

$$\text{syl} \;\rightarrow\; \text{syl\_onset, rhyme}. \tag{6.5}$$

$$\text{rhyme} \;\rightarrow\; \text{short\_vowel, coda}. \tag{6.6}$$
$$\text{rhyme} \;\rightarrow\; \text{long\_vowel, coda}. \tag{6.7}$$
$$\text{rhyme} \;\rightarrow\; \text{long\_vowel}. \tag{6.8}$$

6.4.1. Syllable onsets

Consider the syllable onset first. The broad classes of onset are structured (see Figure 6.2a) as follows:

$$\text{syl\_onset} \;\rightarrow\; \text{v\_onset}. \tag{6.9}$$
$$\text{syl\_onset} \;\rightarrow\; \text{uv\_onset}. \tag{6.10}$$

$$\text{v\_onset} \;\rightarrow\; \text{abr\_onset}. \tag{6.11}$$
$$\text{v\_onset} \;\rightarrow\; \text{cont\_onset}. \tag{6.12}$$

$$\text{uv\_onset} \;\rightarrow\; \text{uvstop1}. \tag{6.13}$$
$$\text{uv\_onset} \;\rightarrow\; \text{uvfric1}. \tag{6.14}$$
$$\text{uv\_onset} \;\rightarrow\; \text{affric1}. \tag{6.15}$$
$$\text{uv\_onset} \;\rightarrow\; \text{t.cluster}. \tag{6.16}$$
$$\text{uv\_onset} \;\rightarrow\; \text{s.cluster}. \tag{6.17}$$

$$\text{abr\_onset} \;\rightarrow\; \text{vstop1}. \tag{6.18}$$
$$\text{abr\_onset} \;\rightarrow\; \text{d.cluster}. \tag{6.19}$$

$$\text{cont\_onset} \;\rightarrow\; \text{vfric}. \tag{6.20}$$
$$\text{cont\_onset} \;\rightarrow\; \text{nlg}. \tag{6.21}$$
$$\text{cont\_onset} \;\rightarrow\; \text{open\_onset}. \tag{6.22}$$

The open onsets, for example <u>ar</u>t, <u>ha</u>rt are simply energy

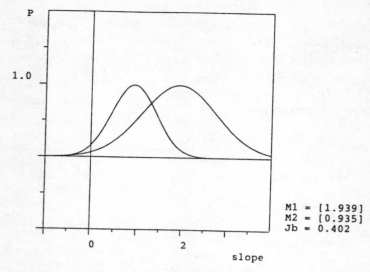

Figure 6.5. Syllable onset slope:
stop-like (M1) and continuant (M2) consonants

onsets.

$$[\texttt{cont\_coda}]\texttt{open\_onset} \ \rightarrow \ \texttt{(med)onset}. \qquad (6.23)$$
$$\texttt{open\_onset} \ \rightarrow \ \texttt{(steep)onset}. \qquad (6.24)$$
$$\texttt{open\_onset} \ \rightarrow \ \texttt{whisper}. \qquad (6.25)$$

$$\texttt{whisper} \ \rightarrow \ \texttt{(steep)onset}. \qquad (6.26)$$

There is no clear contrast between a whispered onset (**h̲art**)
and an open onset (**art**) in terms of the features used.

The stops are classified as voiced or unvoiced on the basis
of the intensity of the high frequency burst at release of the
stop, and the slope of the subsequent onset to the syllabic
peak.

$$\texttt{vstop1} \ \rightarrow \ \texttt{vstop,(steep)onset}. \qquad (6.27)$$
$$\texttt{vstop} \ \rightarrow \ \texttt{(weak\_burst)fric}. \qquad (6.28)$$

```
uvstop1  →  uvstop,(steep)onset .              (6.29)
uvstop  →  (strong_burst)fric.                 (6.30)
[uvfric]uvstop  →  (med_low)dip .              (6.31)
```

The allophones of the stops are generally aspirated in syllable initial position, with unvoiced stops more so than voiced
stops (tar/bar). All the stops have a steep energy onset to
the vowel, in contrast to continuant consonants which are
described as having a medium onset (pay/lay). Figure 6.5
shows the distribution of onset slope for 'steep' and 'med'
(medium) classes of onset. Although the class separation indicated by the plot and the measure J_b is poor, this is just
one contribution to a compound decision-making process in
which all the evidence is considered; sequential class separation is better than isolated class separation due to the effect
of the contextual constraints. The rule (6.31) describes an
elision in which an unvoiced fricative absorbs a subsequent
unvoiced stop (star). Figure 6.6a shows the distribution of
burst duration and intensity for voiced and unvoiced stops.
The decision is primarily based upon the intensity, the degree
of aspiration, as shown in Figure 6.6b. The class separation
using this feature is poor, but can be greatly improved by the
addition of stress and voice onset time (VOT) information.
The stress information is related to the intensity of the subsequent vocalic peak, and the VOT is measured as the duration
between the burst peak and the start of the vocalic segment.
This information can be extracted by mapping the terminal
vectors onto an appropriate sub-space associated with an intermediate category, for example:

```
vstop1  →  (voiced)vstop2 .
vstop2  →  vstop,(steep)onset .
vstop  →  (weak_burst)fric .
```

where a function attached to the rule for 'vstop2' maps the
terminal vectors onto the sub-space associated with category
'vstop2' (see Section 5.4). Measurement vectors consisting

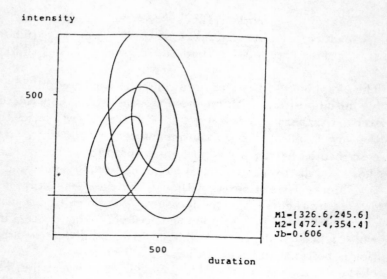

intensity

500

500

duration

M1=[326.6,245.6]
M2=[472.4,354.4]
Jb=0.606

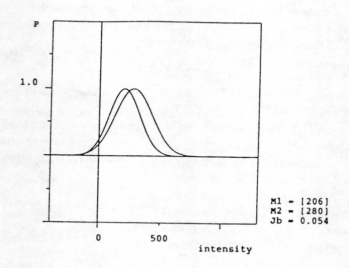

P

1.0

0   500

intensity

M1 = [206]
M2 = [280]
Jb = 0.054

Figure 6.6. Burst intensity for voiced and unvoiced stops
weak burst (M1), strong burst (M2)

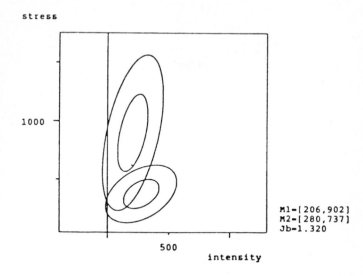

Figure 6.6. continued

of burst intensity, VOT, and stress are classified according to the likelihood function referenced by the qualifier 'voiced'. Figure 6.6c shows distributions for burst intensity and stress for voiced and unvoiced stops. A comparison with the distributions for burst intensity alone illustrate the dramatic improvement in class separation when stress information is included, and this is reflected in the respective inter-class separation measures. The mean values for burst intensity are the same for both Figure 6.6b and Figure 6.6c, but the addition of stress information pulls the distributions apart.

Figure 6.7 shows the voice onset time, and VOT as a function of stress for voiced and unvoiced stops. The decision boundary between the two classes of stop in terms of VOT (Figure 6.7a) occurs at around 40 ms, which is in agreement with results obtained by hand (Eimas, 1981). The stress relationship shown in Figure 6.7b is again effective in increasing the class separation. Figure 6.7c shows the distribution of VOT as Figure 6.7a, but for stressed syllables only. Com-

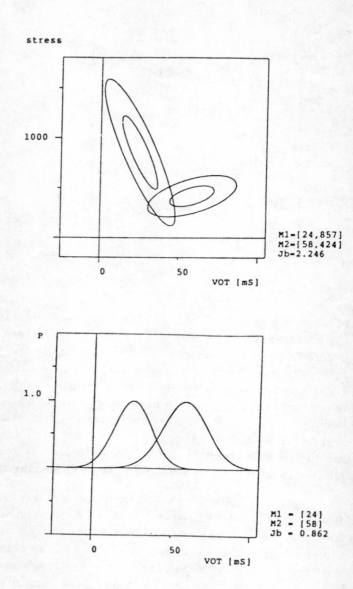

Figure 6.7. Voice onset time for voiced and unvoiced stops weak burst (M1), strong burst (M2)

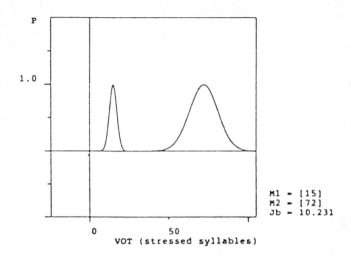

P

1.0

M1 - [15]
M2 - [72]
Jb - 10.231

0   50
VOT (stressed syllables)

Figure 6.7. continued

parison with Figure 6.7a illustrates the result that VOT can be a reliable cue to the voiced/voiceless contrast in stops for stressed syllables.

The fricatives and affricates are classified according to the duration and intensity of the frication, and the slope of the subsequent onset to the syllabic peak.

$$uvfric1 \rightarrow uvfric,(med)onset. \qquad (6.32)$$
$$uvfric \rightarrow (strong\_fric)fric. \qquad (6.33)$$
$$uvfric[uvstop] \rightarrow (med\_fric)fric. \qquad (6.34)$$

$$vfric1 \rightarrow vfric,(med)onset. \qquad (6.35)$$
$$vfric \rightarrow (weak\_fric)fric. \qquad (6.36)$$

$$affric1 \rightarrow affric,(steep)onset. \qquad (6.37)$$
$$affric \rightarrow (med\_fric)fric. \qquad (6.38)$$

Frication, associated with fricatives and affricates, is con-

189

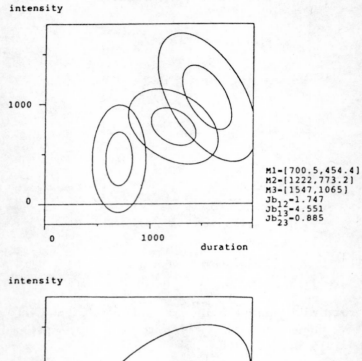

intensity

1000

0

0   1000   duration

M1=[700.5,454.4]
M2=[1222,773.2]
M3=[1547,1065]
Jb_{12}=1.747
Jb_{13}=4.551
Jb_{23}=0.885

intensity

1000

0

0   1000   duration

M1=[402.8,302.5]
M2=[1171,776.7]
Jb=1.552

Figure 6.8. Classes of frication
(a) burst (M1), fric (M2)
(b) weak fric (M1), med fric (M2), strong fric (M3)

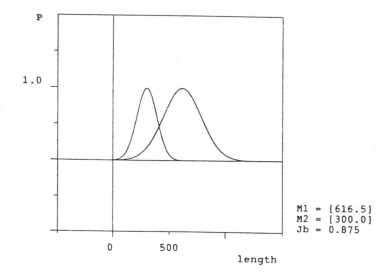

Figure 6.9. Initial (M1) and initial reduced (M2)
nasal, liquid, glide

sidered a separate category of high frequency event, distinguished from the category of bursts, associated with the stops, by the duration of frication. Figure 6.8a shows the distributions across all classes of the respective categories 'fric' and 'burst', in terms of duration and intensity. The category 'fric' (or more precisely the feature space associated with the category 'fric') is qualified by three classes of frication: 'weak', 'med' (i.e. medium), and 'strong', and the distributions of these classes is shown in Figure 6.8b.

The frication associated with syllable initial allophones is generally longer and stronger than the corresponding allophones in syllable coda position, (<u>s</u>ick/ki<u>ss</u>, <u>z</u>ip/bi<u>z</u>, <u>ch</u>ick/ki<u>tch</u>), and this is reflected by the respective class separations in Figure 6.8b.

Rule (6.34) represents the reduction of an unvoiced fricative by a following unvoiced stop (<u>s</u>ay/<u>st</u>ay). The distinction between unvoiced fricative and affricate is based upon the duration of frication, but this contrast disappears when the duration of an unvoiced fricative is reduced. It can be seen that the intensity information does not significantly contribute to the decision in this case. It turns out to be difficult to classify voiced fricatives in terms of the selected features. The quality of voicing is erratic and it is difficult to align the frication event correctly. In general, results for voiced frication were poor.

Nasals liquids and glides are generally indistinguishable in terms of the features used, but the class of 'nlg' (i.e. nasal or liquid or glide) is identified by the presence of a 'pfoot' in the 'onset', or by a reduction in sonority following a continuant coda.

```
nlg1   →  nlg,(med)onset.                    (6.39)
nlg    →  (long)pfoot.                        (6.40)
[uvfric]nlg  →  (short)pfoot.                 (6.41)
[cont_coda]nlg  →  (med_high)dip.             (6.42)
```

Rule (6.41) describes the reduction of a 'nlg' by an unvoiced fricative (pass me, hiss loudly). Figure 6.9 shows the classes of 'pfoot' as distributions of 'nlg' and reduced 'nlg' categories, in terms of the 'pfoot' length.

Initial stop clusters are CCV consonant clusters which are introduced by a voiced or unvoiced stop, as defined in rules (6.28) and (6.30) respectively, and broadly followed by a reduced 'lg' (i.e. liquid or glide) category.

```
d.cluster  →  vstop,lg.                       (6.43)
t.cluster  →  uvstop,lg.                       (6.44)

lg  →  (short)pfoot,(med)onset.               (6.45)
```

The reduced 'lg' in rule (6.45) is characteristic of 'lg' in initial stop clusters. Compare, for example, with the initial 'nlg' category in rule (6.40) (<u>l</u>ay/p<u>l</u>ay).

Initial fricative clusters are CCV or CCCV consonant clusters denoted by the generic symbol 's.cluster' (see Figure 6.3b).

s.cluster	→ uvfric,s.cluster1.	(6.46)

s.cluster1	→ nlg,(med)onset.	(6.47)
s.cluster1	→ uvstop,s.cluster2.	(6.48)

s.cluster2	→ (steep)onset.	(6.49)
s.cluster2	→ liquid,(med)onset.	(6.50)

liquid	→ (short)pfoot.	(6.51)

Reduction of the initial unvoiced fricative prior to an unvoiced stop (<u>st</u>ail/<u>sn</u>ail) is part of the rule for unvoiced fricatives (6.34). The reduction of a 'nlg' in second consonant position is part of the rule for 'nlg' (6.41). The elision of an unvoiced stop in second consonant position, due to the initial unvoiced fricative, is part of the rule for 'uvstop' (6.31).

6.4.2. Vowels

The vowels are classified simply as either short or long, depending upon duration and stress. In the context of a post-vocalic unvoiced consonant the inherent duration of a vowel is reduced, and with a voiced consonant it is lengthened.

short_vowel[uv_coda]	→ (short)peak.	(6.52)
short_vowel[v_coda]	→ (med)peak.	(6.53)

long_vowel[uv_coda]	→ (long)peak.	(6.54)
long_vowel[v_coda]	→ (extralong)peak.	(6.55)

Figure 6.10a shows the distribution of vowel durations for the four classes of peak, and Figure 6.10b shows the vowel

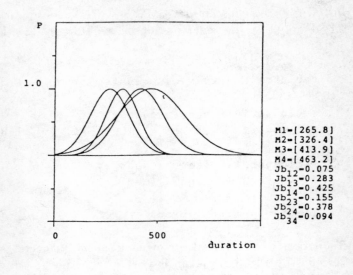

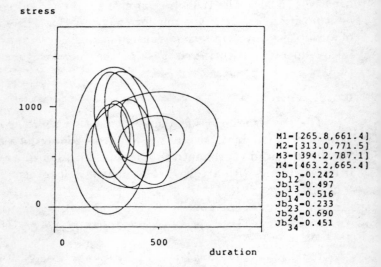

Figure 6.10. Classes of peak:
short (M1), med (M2), long (M3), extralong (M4)

durations with the stress-related intensity feature. These results show that the vowel duration is not particularly correlated with vowel intensity, and that the stress information does little to improve a poor class separation. Therefore it is concluded that, unlike the results for isolated words given in Chapter 2, the shortening-lengthening rule and vowel durations in general are not an invariant cue to vowel class in continuous speech; there is too much latitude for durational variation. However, classification of vowels in isolation is not the goal, and vowel duration is a useful component which contributes evidence for composite reasoning, particularly when the decision rests upon a short/long vowel contrast (pa̲rty/pa̲tty). Figure 6.11 illustrates the class separation of inherently short and long vowels, irrespective of context. Again it can be seen that stress information does not contribute directly to decisions based upon vowel duration, at least in terms of the measurements made here.

6.4.3. Syllable codas

The broad classes of coda are structured as follows (see Figure 6.2b):

$$coda \rightarrow v\_coda. \tag{6.56}$$
$$coda \rightarrow uv\_coda. \tag{6.57}$$

$$v\_coda \rightarrow abr\_coda. \tag{6.58}$$
$$v\_coda \rightarrow cont\_coda. \tag{6.59}$$

$$uv\_coda \rightarrow uvstop2. \tag{6.60}$$
$$uv\_coda \rightarrow uvfric2. \tag{6.61}$$
$$uv\_coda \rightarrow affric2. \tag{6.62}$$
$$uv\_coda \rightarrow nt.cluster. \tag{6.63}$$
$$uv\_coda \rightarrow st.cluster. \tag{6.64}$$
$$uv\_coda \rightarrow ts.cluster. \tag{6.65}$$

$$abr\_coda \rightarrow vstop2. \tag{6.66}$$
$$abr\_coda \rightarrow zd.cluster. \tag{6.67}$$

195

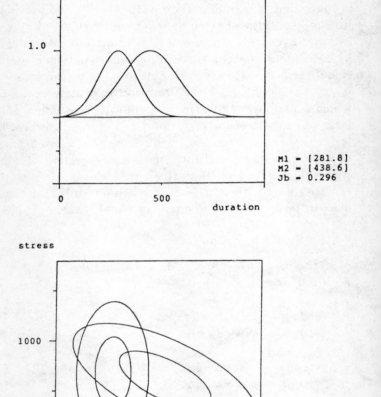

Figure 6.11. Inherent vowel durations
short (M1), long (M2)

$$abr\_coda \; \rightarrow \; nd.cluster. \hspace{2cm} (6.68)$$

$$cont\_coda \; \rightarrow \; vfric2. \hspace{2.5cm} (6.69)$$
$$cont\_coda \; \rightarrow \; nl2. \hspace{3cm} (6.70)$$
$$cont\_coda \; \rightarrow \; ng2. \hspace{3cm} (6.71)$$
$$cont\_coda \; \rightarrow \; dz.cluster. \hspace{2cm} (6.72)$$
$$cont\_coda \; \rightarrow \; nz.cluster. \hspace{2cm} (6.73)$$

The stops are identified by a steep energy offset from the preceding sonorant peak, followed by a brief silence during the closure.

$$vstop2 \; \rightarrow \; (steep)offset,vstop. \hspace{1.3cm} (6.74)$$
$$vstop \; \rightarrow \; (short\_low)dip. \hspace{1.6cm} (6.75)$$
$$vstop[open\_onset] \; \rightarrow \; (short\_low)dip,$$
$$(weak\_burst)fric. \hspace{0.5cm} (6.76)$$

$$uvstop2 \; \rightarrow \; (steep)offset,uvstop. \hspace{0.8cm} (6.77)$$
$$uvstop \; \rightarrow \; (med\_low)dip. \hspace{1.7cm} (6.78)$$
$$uvstop[open\_onset] \; \rightarrow \; (med\_low)dip,$$
$$(weak\_burst)fric. \hspace{0.5cm} (6.79)$$

The release of final stops is restricted to the case of a following open onset (di̲d all). Both voiced and unvoiced stops are qualified in the same way for this context, as a compromise intended to cover both aspirated and flapped stops (hi̲t it/hi̲d it).

The stops have a characteristically steep energy offset from the syllabic peak, which contrasts with the 'med' (medium) energy offset associated with continuant consonants. Figure 6.12 shows the distribution of offset slope for the classes 'steep' and 'med'. Comparison with Figure 6.5 shows that in general the slopes of energy onset and offset contribute relatively invariant class-conditional information. Comparison with Figure 6.10 shows that onset and offset slope are generally rather less variant measures than peak duration. This is to be expected since there is less latitude

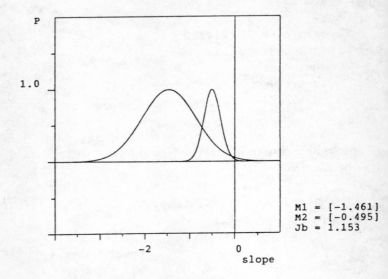

Figure 6.12. Syllable offset slope
stop-like (M1), continuant (M2) consonants

for articulatory variation in the production of energy onsets
and offsets than there is for a sustained vocalic peak.

The voiced/voiceless contrast in final stops is indicated
by the duration of the closure, and by the intensity of the
release prior to an open onset, (hi<u>t</u> all/hi<u>d</u> all). Figure
6.10 shows the contrast between voiced and unvoiced final
stops in terms of the closure duration. A complete closure
is indicated by a '(low)dip', as illustrated by the distribution of intensity and duration in Figure 6.13b. A 'low' is a
class of energy dip distinct from the 'high(dip)' which is
characteristic of the inter-vocalic 'nlg' category. The distribution of 'low' and 'high' classes of 'dip' is shown in
Figure 6.13c.

The fricatives and affricates are identified by the presence of
frication over a substantial duration, with the affricates ex-
hibiting a "stop-like" closure.

uvfric2 → (med)offset,uvfric.   (6.80)
uvfric → (med_fric)fric.   (6.81)

vfric2 → (med)offset,(long)nfoot,vfric. (6.82)
vfric2[cont_onset] → (med)offset,
                              (med_high)dip,vfric. (6.83)

vfric → (weak_fric)fric.   (6.84)

affric2 → (steep)offset,affric.   (6.85)
affric → (med_low)dip,(weak_fric)fric.   (6.86)

Final frication is generally shorter and weaker than initial frication. This is represented declaratively by the respective qualifiers to the category 'fric' in rules (6.33) and (6.81) for the example of unvoiced frication. The allophonic variation of the unvoiced fricative /s/ is a particularly valuable cue to syllabification, since this phoneme is a constituent of many consonant clusters, and the position of the juncture will often be phonotactically ambiguous (pea stalks/peace talks). The class separation upon which the syllabification decision rests is shown in Figure 6.8b. Among the unvoiced fricatives, the phoneme /s/ is the most prominent in terms of the features used. The single high-frequency energy contour is insufficient to capture both /s/ and /sh/ (as in "show"), since the characteristic resonance associated with /sh/ is rather lower than for /s/, being in the region 3 to 4 kHz. The weak unvoiced fricative /f/ (as in "few") is also difficult to detect in terms of the features used. Voiced frication is difficult to identify, primarily because the segmentation of such mixed voiced and frication events is unreliable in terms of the features used.

Nasals and liquids. There are no final glides, and so the final semi-sonorant category is restricted to 'nl' (i.e. nasal or liquid) and the /ng/ phoneme, (as in ring).

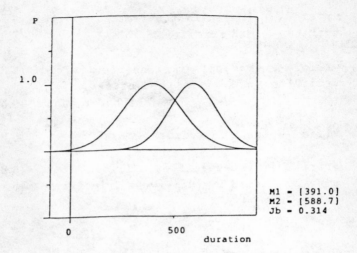

M1 - [391.0]
M2 - [588.7]
Jb - 0.314

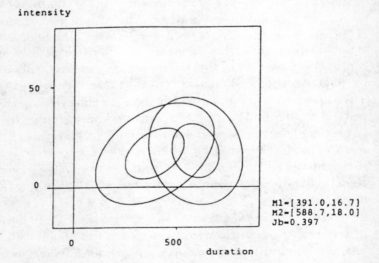

M1-[391.0,16.7]
M2-[588.7,18.0]
Jb-0.397

Figure 6.13. Closures and energy dips
(a) (b) short low dip (M1), med low dip (M2)
(c) low dip (M1), high dip (M2)

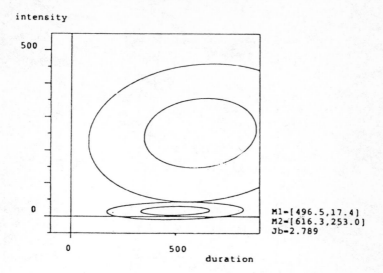

Figure 6.13. continued

$$nl2 \rightarrow (med)offset, nl. \qquad (6.87)$$
$$nl \rightarrow (med\_high)dip. \qquad (6.88)$$
$$nl \rightarrow (med)nfoot. \qquad (6.89)$$
$$nl[uv\_onset] \rightarrow (short)nfoot. \qquad (6.90)$$
$$nl[uv\_tail] \rightarrow (short)nfoot. \qquad (6.91)$$

$$[short\_vowel]ng2 \rightarrow (med)offset,ng. \qquad (6.92)$$
$$ng \rightarrow (long)nfoot. \qquad (6.93)$$

Final 'nl' is longer than its syllable initial counterpart, but is
reduced by a following unvoiced consonant (under/hunter).
This does not adversely effect the syllabification, because the
juncture is indicated by the foot slope; final 'nl' has an
'nfoot', initial 'nlg' has a 'pfoot'. Provided the segmentation identifies a "foot" in the energy contour, then syllabification follows from structural constraints, (bean ice/be
nice). Rule (6.91) is included to meet the requirements for final nasal consonant clusters (see rule (6.100)). The phoneme

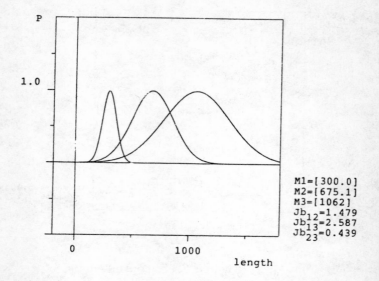

Figure 6.14. Post-vocalic nasal, liquid
reduced nl (M1), nl (M2), ng (M3)

/ng/ is phonotactically constrained to follow a short vowel,
and is distinguished by the lengthened 'nfoot', following
the initial offset of energy from the vowel, (ran past/rang
past). Figure 6.14 shows the distribution of the final 'nl'
category, in terms of the length of the 'nfoot', for the 'nl'
category, its reduced allophone, and the 'ng' category.

Final stop clusters consist of a stop followed by a fricative
with voicing agreement.

$$ts.cluster \rightarrow (steep)offset,uvstop,uvfric \quad (6.94)$$

$$dz.cluster \rightarrow (steep)offset,vstop,vfric. \quad (6.95)$$

Final fricative clusters consist of a fricative followed by a
stop with voicing agreement.

$$\text{st.cluster} \rightarrow \text{(med)offset,uvfric,uvstop.} \quad (6.96)$$

$$\text{zd.cluster} \rightarrow \text{(med)offset,vfric,vstop.} \quad (6.97)$$

Final nasal clusters consist of a nasal followed by a stop, a fricative, or an affricate. The representation necessarily divides the categories of cluster in order to comply with the general structure for voiced/unvoiced codas and continuant/abrupt codas.

$$\text{nd.cluster} \rightarrow \text{(med)offset,nl,vstop.} \quad (6.98)$$

$$\text{nz.cluster} \rightarrow \text{(med)offset,nl,vfric.} \quad (6.99)$$

$$\text{nt.cluster} \rightarrow \text{(med)offset,nl,uv\_tail.} \quad (6.100)$$

$$\text{uv\_tail} \rightarrow \text{uvstop.} \quad (6.101)$$
$$\text{uv\_tail} \rightarrow \text{uvfric.} \quad (6.102)$$
$$\text{uv\_tail} \rightarrow \text{affric.} \quad (6.103)$$

The 'uv_tail' constituent represents categories which reduce the duration of preceding nasals, (ben̲d/ben̲t, pen̲s/pen̲ce, pin̲s/pin̲ch), (see rule (6.91)).

6.5. Recognition results

The hybrid classifier described in Sections 5.3 and 5.4, with the syllable grammar described above (and listed in Appendix 1), was trained on a set of utterances (see Appendix 2), segmented using the procedure described in section 4.5. The machine was then set to recognize a different set of test data (Appendix 2). The confusion matrix of Figure 6.15 shows the recognition results for each broad phonetic category, based upon test data which was correctly segmented. The input categories, (the true state of the phonetic constituents), are listed in the left column. The corresponding numbers to the right of the last column are the number of instances of each category in the test data. The entries along

203

each row give the number of instances of test data classified as the output category listed along the top row.

The cluster of entries in the top left of the figure illustrates the structural similarity between the initial stops, fricatives, and affricates, in terms of the features used. The separation between these classes is aided by the compound decision which takes both the the quality of frication and the slope of the energy onset to the vowel into consideration. In particular, initial stops are well separated when the stress information of the following vowel and the voice onset time is incorporated. This information improves the recognition rate to over 90% from 60% when burst intensity alone is used.

It is concluded that information such as burst intensity related to stress, VOT, and energy onset slope combine to form a relatively invariant cue to the contrast between these structurally similar classes. The contrast is particularly marked for stressed syllables. This is a great improvement on the corresponding result given in Chapter 2. Given that the structure of these classes, in terms of their elementary segment strings, is also one of the more successful segmentations, then these simple features are promising cues to syllable initial manner of articulation.

The cluster of entries in the matrix of Figure 6.15 which correspond to the syllable final stops and affricates illustrates another group of classes with a structural similarity. The final affricate is distinguished by the relatively long duration of frication, on average 70 ms, following the stop-like closure. The contrast between final stops is solely due to the duration of the closure, and consequently the class separation between final voiced and unvoiced stops is not so good as for their syllable initial counterparts. The addition of stress information does not seem to improve the contrast in this case. Nevertheless the contrast based upon closure duration can provide the fine detail required to discriminate between similar words, such as "rabbit/rapid".

Confusion between initial and final stops and affricates

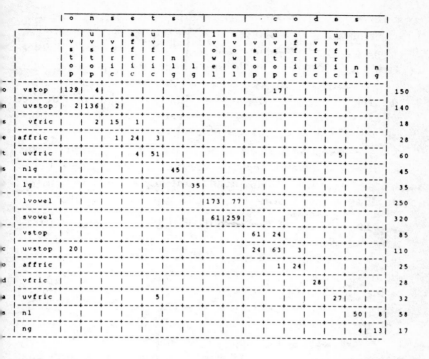

Figure 6.15. Confusion matrix of broad phonetic classes

is the result of an ambiguous syllabic juncture. The grammar constrains this to occur only for sequences of long-vowel, released-obstruent, and vowel (e.g. p<u>ar</u>t <u>of</u>). All syllables with short vowels, or with unreleased final stop consonants, bind the post-vocalic consonant to themselves. All other sequences may situate the syllabic juncture either side of the released stop. Of this type of sequence, final unvoiced stops and initial voiced stops are ambiguous according to the grammar, as are final affricates and initial unvoiced stops. The results for stops and fricatives are much better if the syllabification error is not considered, and they are excellent if the voiced/unvoiced distinction is not made.

The contrast between initial and final unvoiced fricatives is relatively strong provided the initial fricative is not reduced. The intensity and duration of these allophones provides a strong cue to the position of the syllabic juncture, as in "there's#no/there#snow". The average duration of initial /s/, for example, is about 150 ms, and final /s/ is 120 ms. In the case of reduced initial unvoiced fricatives, as in "<u>s</u>talk", the syllabification cue depends more upon the closure duration associated with the stop. For example the contrast between "pea#stalks" and "peace#talks" is cued primarily by the closure duration; the intensity and duration of the /s/ in this case is not so contrastive.

The syllabic juncture position with respect to an inter-vocalic nasal or liquid depends upon the segmentation. If a 'pfoot' or 'nfoot' segment is present, then syllabification is unambiguous. If the inter-vocalic segment is simply a '(med_high)dip', then the juncture position may be either side of the liquid or nasal. In this case its position depends solely upon the binding rule associated with the length of the first syllable vowel.

In the cases where the juncture is positioned with respect to a nasal or liquid and at least one other consonant, then the syllabification is structurally unambiguous. In general, syllabification is aided by consonant clusters. The strong phonotactic constraints, applied to the structural detail in consonant clusters, produce reliable decisions on the positions of syllabic junctures.

Final nasals, liquids, and the /ng/ phoneme are structurally similar, but the duration of the associated nfoot segment cues a contrast between them, as is shown by the corresponding entries in Figure 6.15.

Vowel durations do not appear to be an invariant cue to vowel classes based upon inherent durations. The addition of stress information does not appear to improve the contrast. The shortening/lengthening rule associated with the quality of voicing of the following consonant is not nearly so reliable for continuous speech as it was shown to be for isolated words in Chapter 2. One reason for this is the measurement of the vowel duration, based only upon the peak segment, which does not describe vowel duration successfully. It is expected that the durational contrast for vowels will improve with a better definition of duration. Certainly the addition of formant information, will greatly benefit vowel classification, and the extraction of such information is facilitated by the identification of the vocalic peak.

The chief drawback of this model, using the simple features described, is the reliance upon an initial segmentation. Failures in segmentation are segment sequences which are not accounted for in the grammar. For example, the omission of a 'pfoot' or 'nfoot' where a syllable initial or final 'nl' category is supposed to be, or conversely the inclusion of an 'nfoot' or 'pfoot' where an abrupt 'onset' or 'offset' is expected. In a number of cases syllable final stops were released (e.g. last part) although the grammar describes this occurrence only for final stops preceding an open onset. In one case the release of a voiced stop (did) was so pronounced as to resemble an additional syllable (dinner) in terms of the segments of the low frequency energy contour. Syllabic artifacts are also generated by "quavering" over long vowels, which introduces spurious energy dips. In the high

207

frequency energy contour, segmentation failure is caused by the absence of the frication burst associated with syllable initial stops. Conversely, and more commonly, the presence of apparent substantial frication due to general spectral tilt or an especially high third formant (e.g. for initial liquids) also leads to segmentation errors. As has been mentioned, voiced fricatives are a problem in terms of the features used. These segmentation errors are dependent upon the segmentation procedure, and in turn upon the signal analysis and feature extraction, rather than the syllabic model. Although in many cases it would be possible to account for segmentation errors by the addition of error correcting productions to the grammar, this is generally not a worthwhile exercise; further complexity and ambiguity is generated, with no guarantee that the problem is definitively solved. Rather, it is necessary to re-examine the analysis and feature extraction, and to introduce additional features to characterize robust segments.

The results achieved by the syllabic model are promising considering the simplicity of the features used. The utilization of phonotactic and allophonic constraints is shown to be an important factor in the reduction of complexity and the identification of less variant categories. The hybrid machine is shown to provide a vehicle for the comprehensible representation of linguistic constraints, and a process of evidential reasoning capable of integrating evidence from diverse acoustic cues. The broad phonetic transcription is sufficiently detailed to discriminate similar utterances, and combined with the implicit syllabification, this is expected to reduce the problem of lexical access.

CHAPTER 7
Conclusion

Speaker independent recognition of continuous speech requires a signal-to-symbol classification process over a sequence of symbols. The numerical characteristics of any symbol vary widely according to speaker, and according to the linguistic context. Using a sequential computer, we are obliged to find, in some optimal sense, a *summary* of this variation, and a practical account of the variance due to speaker and linguistic context.

The summary description of the numerical variation of speech pattern classes is incorporated into a pattern classification model which may be based upon a geometric, topological, or probabilistic interpretation of patterns (see Section 5.2). These methods are closely related in a strong sense, as the respective decision rules can all be seen as defining decision surfaces to partition a feature space. We see that for topological decision rules, the decision surfaces between pattern classes are essentially linear. For probabilistic decision rules, unless the covariance matrices are diagonal, the decision surfaces are hyper-quadratic.

These classification methods based upon low-order decision surfaces are necessarily simple so that the parameter estimation problem (ie training) is tractable. The methods are also, in a strong sense, well adapted to the classification of patterns derived from stationary signals in zero-mean additive white noise. We have seen in Chapter 4 how judicious feature selection and extraction, with the transformations of the feature space described in Chapter 5, can optimize the performance of such classifiers from the viewpoint of intra-class variance, and also inter-class distance.

The speech signal is of course non-stationary, and the noise statistics also vary widely. This presents an enormous problem to the sequential computer, and in speech processing this problem has been approached using the idea of sequential pattern classification. In this approach it is assumed that the speech signal is a concatenation of relatively stationary segments, each of which can be classified in a conventional manner, using a method based on the principles described in Section 5.2. Composite models may be constructed from sequences of such segments, and a compound decision may then classify observation sequences. Examples of this approach are the whole-word models defined in terms of templates or hidden Markov models as described in Chapter 3.

In this book we have described how some of the problems associated with whole-word pattern matching in connected speech recognition can be approached using a principled subdivision of words into syllable structures. Given a structural model by which articulation classes may be combined to form syllables, which are ultimately combined to form words, we have a far more economical representation of a vocabulary. In addition it is possible to explicitly model coarticulatory effects at word boundaries, and so forth. The syllable based model is designed to improve the performance of the pattern-matching components, while the overheads of combining the sequential elements are kept to a minimum. In Chapter 3 we argued that, lacking adequate inferrence procedures, *a priori* knowledge in the form of principled linguistic theory should be employed to design the structural component of a composite model, if the model is to converge onto some kind of optimality. In Chapter 5 we described a hybrid sequential pattern classification machine which can search through a set of symbol sequences, making optimal sequential decisions, to arrive at a final decision on the basis of maximum likelihood, with respect to the model parameters estimated from training data. This machine provides a practical method for implementing speech knowledge, and a tool for experimentation with integrated acoustic cues, with the aim of finding less-variant correlates to elementary linguistic constituents.

We have seen in Chapter 4 that the important properties of the initial signal analysis and extraction of speech parameters are that the transformation is data reducing and information preserving. In practice the transformation must also be computationally efficient. This transformation is an initial "hard" decision based on a concept of information preservation which is realized in terms of a simple model of idealized patterns. It is therefore not necessarily perfectly adapted for the analysis of continuous speech signals. It would be convenient, for example, if the transformation makes less-variant acoustic correlates explicit in the new signal representation.

There is much evidence in favour of invariant speech signal properties. Experiments with infant speech perception (Eimas, 1981) clearly demonstrate that fine phonetic contrasts, such as the place of articulation for a particular manner class, are detected in the absense of all higher-level information. A first step towards understanding this process is then to experiment with signal representations based upon the human auditory system (Lyon, 1982; Seneff, 1985). It is reasonable to assume that human speech and the human auditory transformation are, to some degree, specifically adapted to suit each other. A signal representation derived from the auditory transformation should make explicit less-variant correlates which can be traced directly back to their original articulatory gestures.

The methods described in this book are adapted to the constraints imposed by a finite memory sequential computer. In particular we have described how the recognition process can be decomposed into a sequence of steps, with the aim of progressive data reduction towards a final symbolic representation. However the human brain is not a sequential machine; in terms of computer architecture it is massively parallel. It is therefore of great interest to consider recent developments in pattern recognition methods which are adapted to parallel machines (Rumelhart and McClelland, 1986).

Pattern recognition based upon parallel distributed processing enables high-resolution non-parametric classification without extensive data reduction or any prior assumptions by decomposing the pattern into an array of inter-connected parallel decision-making units. These arrays are organized as layers, with each successive layer a refinement of the previous. The processing units within one layer are inter-connected by weights which specify the degree of influence a decision at one unit has over the decision at another. These weights represent a large number of *weak constraints* which are simultaneously satisfied by a process of decision propagation through the network of units. This propagation of decisions should settle into an equilibrium which is characteristic of the input pattern. The learning procedure (Hinton *et al*, 1984) is a hill-climbing technique which progressively modifies the weights so as to optimize an information theoretic measure of how effectively the weights in the network model the structure of the patterns.

The great advantage of this approach is that the recognition process can be decomposed into the satisfaction of a large number of weak constraints, operating in a relatively autonomous fashion, and yet arrive at an optimal compound decision. However, this approach is very slow if simulated on a sequential computer, and awaits the arrival of suitable parallel machines.

Appendix 1

The syllable grammar described in Chapter 6 is listed below.

Syllable sequences

phrase	→ syl, pause, phrase.	(1)
phrase	→ ∅.	(2)
pause	→ (long_low)dip.	(3)
pause	→ ∅.	(4)

Syllable structure

syl	→ syl_onset, rhyme.	(5)
rhyme	→ short_vowel, coda.	(6)
rhyme	→ long_vowel, coda.	(7)
rhyme	→ long_vowel.	(8)

Syllable onsets

syl_onset	→ v_onset.	(9)
syl_onset	→ uv_onset.	(10)
v_onset	→ abr_onset.	(11)
v_onset	→ cont_onset.	(12)
uv_onset	→ uvstop1.	(13)
uv_onset	→ uvfric1.	(14)

$$uv\_onset \rightarrow affric1. \tag{15}$$
$$uv\_onset \rightarrow t.cluster. \tag{16}$$
$$uv\_onset \rightarrow s.cluster. \tag{17}$$

$$abr\_onset \rightarrow vstop1. \tag{18}$$
$$abr\_onset \rightarrow d.cluster. \tag{19}$$

$$cont\_onset \rightarrow vfric. \tag{20}$$
$$cont\_onset \rightarrow nlg. \tag{21}$$
$$cont\_onset \rightarrow open\_onset. \tag{22}$$

Open onsets

$$[cont\_coda]open\_onset \rightarrow (med)onset. \tag{23}$$
$$open\_onset \rightarrow (steep)onset. \tag{24}$$
$$open\_onset \rightarrow whisper. \tag{25}$$

$$whisper \rightarrow (steep)onset. \tag{26}$$

Initial stop consonants

$$vstop1 \rightarrow vstop,(steep)onset. \tag{27}$$
$$vstop \rightarrow (weak\_burst)fric. \tag{28}$$

$$uvstop1 \rightarrow uvstop,(steep)onset. \tag{29}$$
$$uvstop \rightarrow (strong\_burst)fric. \tag{30}$$
$$[uvfric]uvstop \rightarrow (med\_low)dip. \tag{31}$$

Initial fricatives and affricates

$$uvfric1 \rightarrow uvfric,(med)onset. \tag{32}$$
$$uvfric \rightarrow (strong\_fric)fric. \tag{33}$$
$$uvfric[uvstop] \rightarrow (med\_fric)fric. \tag{34}$$

$$vfric1 \rightarrow vfric,(med)onset. \tag{35}$$
$$vfric \rightarrow (weak\_fric)fric. \tag{36}$$

214

$$\text{affric1} \rightarrow \text{affric,(steep)onset.} \tag{37}$$
$$\text{affric} \rightarrow \text{(med\_fric)fric.} \tag{38}$$

Initial nasals liquids and glides

$$\text{nlg1} \rightarrow \text{nlg,(med)onset.} \tag{39}$$
$$\text{nlg} \rightarrow \text{(long)pfoot.} \tag{40}$$
$$\text{[uvfric]nlg} \rightarrow \text{(short)pfoot.} \tag{41}$$
$$\text{[cont\_coda]nlg} \rightarrow \text{(med\_high)dip.} \tag{42}$$

Initial stop clusters

$$\text{d.cluster} \rightarrow \text{vstop,lg.} \tag{43}$$
$$\text{t.cluster} \rightarrow \text{uvstop,lg.} \tag{44}$$

$$\text{lg} \rightarrow \text{(short)pfoot,(med)onset.} \tag{45}$$

Initial fricative clusters

$$\text{s.cluster} \rightarrow \text{uvfric,s.cluster1.} \tag{46}$$

$$\text{s.cluster1} \rightarrow \text{nlg,(med)onset.} \tag{47}$$
$$\text{s.cluster1} \rightarrow \text{uvstop,s.cluster2.} \tag{48}$$

$$\text{s.cluster2} \rightarrow \text{(steep)onset.} \tag{49}$$
$$\text{s.cluster2} \rightarrow \text{liquid,(med)onset.} \tag{50}$$

$$\text{liquid} \rightarrow \text{(short)pfoot.} \tag{51}$$

Vowels

$$\text{short\_vowel[uv\_coda]} \rightarrow \text{(short)peak.} \tag{52}$$
$$\text{short\_vowel[v\_coda]} \rightarrow \text{(med)peak.} \tag{53}$$

$$\text{long\_vowel[uv\_coda]} \rightarrow \text{(long)peak.} \tag{54}$$
$$\text{long\_vowel[v\_coda]} \rightarrow \text{(extralong)peak.} \tag{55}$$

Syllable codas

$$coda \rightarrow v\_coda. \qquad (56)$$
$$coda \rightarrow uv\_coda. \qquad (57)$$

$$v\_coda \rightarrow abr\_coda. \qquad (58)$$
$$v\_coda \rightarrow cont\_coda. \qquad (59)$$

$$uv\_coda \rightarrow uvstop2. \qquad (60)$$
$$uv\_coda \rightarrow uvfric2. \qquad (61)$$
$$uv\_coda \rightarrow affric2. \qquad (62)$$
$$uv\_coda \rightarrow nt.cluster. \qquad (63)$$
$$uv\_coda \rightarrow st.cluster. \qquad (64)$$
$$uv\_coda \rightarrow ts.cluster. \qquad (65)$$

$$abr\_coda \rightarrow vstop2. \qquad (66)$$
$$abr\_coda \rightarrow zd.cluster. \qquad (67)$$
$$abr\_coda \rightarrow nd.cluster. \qquad (68)$$

$$cont\_coda \rightarrow vfric2. \qquad (69)$$
$$cont\_coda \rightarrow nl2. \qquad (70)$$
$$cont\_coda \rightarrow ng2. \qquad (71)$$
$$cont\_coda \rightarrow dz.cluster. \qquad (72)$$
$$cont\_coda \rightarrow nz.cluster. \qquad (73)$$

Final stops

$$vstop2 \rightarrow (steep)offset,vstop. \qquad (74)$$
$$vstop \rightarrow (short\_low)dip. \qquad (75)$$
$$vstop[open\_onset] \rightarrow (short\_low)dip,$$
$$(weak\_burst)fric. \quad (76)$$

$$uvstop2 \rightarrow (steep)offset,uvstop. \qquad (77)$$
$$uvstop \rightarrow (med\_low)dip. \qquad (78)$$
$$uvstop[open\_onset] \rightarrow (med\_low)dip,$$
$$(weak\_burst)fric. \quad (79)$$

Final fricatives and affricates

```
uvfric2 → (med)offset,uvfric.                    (80)
uvfric → (med_fric)fric.                          (81)

vfric2 → (med)offset,(long)nfoot,vfric.          (82)
vfric2[cont_onset] → (med)offset,
                        (med_high)dip,vfric.     (83)

vfric → (weak_fric)fric.                          (84)

affric2 → (steep)offset,affric.                   (85)
affric → (med_low)dip,(weak_fric)fric.            (86)
```

Final nasals and liquids

```
nl2 → (med)offset, nl.                            (87)
nl → (med_high)dip.                               (88)
nl → (med)nfoot.                                  (89)
nl[uv_onset] → (short)nfoot.                       (90)
nl[uv_tail] → (short)nfoot.                         (91)

[short_vowel]ng2 → (med)offset,ng.                 (92)
ng → (long)nfoot.                                   (93)
```

Final stop clusters

```
ts.cluster → (steep)offset,uvstop,uvfric. (94)

dz.cluster → (steep)offset,vstop,vfric.   (95)
```

Final fricative clusters

```
st.cluster → (med)offset,uvfric,uvstop.   (96)

zd.cluster → (med)offset,vfric,vstop.     (97)
```

Final nasal clusters

$$\texttt{nd.cluster} \rightarrow \texttt{(med)offset,nl,vstop}. \tag{98}$$

$$\texttt{nz.cluster} \rightarrow \texttt{(med)offset,nl,vfric}. \tag{99}$$

$$\texttt{nt.cluster} \rightarrow \texttt{(med)offset,nl,uv\_tail}. \tag{100}$$

$$\texttt{uv\_tail} \rightarrow \texttt{uvstop}. \tag{101}$$
$$\texttt{uv\_tail} \rightarrow \texttt{uvfric}. \tag{102}$$
$$\texttt{uv\_tail} \rightarrow \texttt{affric}. \tag{103}$$

Appendix 2

The training data used to estimate the model parameters are listed below. The phrases were spoken by five males, without special attention to speaker rate, stress and accent. All the speakers have a typical southern British dialect (received pronounciation). The recordings were made in a sound-proof "quiet" room. The speech was sampled at 10 kHz, and digitised into 12-bit samples.

Did you see her on the ship.
Pretty Polly took two pennies.
The last part of the chart.
Planet mars cannot be parsed.
Betty tipped her bucket on the red floor.
Johns transistor has two leads.
Bipity bopity boo.
Lots of bits and bobs.
Even boys can spit.
Red leather yellow leather.
Be true tin can.
Beetroot in can.
Shoot the rabbits on a log.
Shoot the rapids on a log.
Pea stalks grow tall.
Peace talks are the thing.
Did Church say that.
Say that again.
Peter missed supper again.

There's no ball like a snowball.
Did you ring sir.
The wolf blew down the garage.
Can Ted play bridge.

The experimental procedure was as follows. The 23 sentences were spoken four times by each of the five speakers. The resulting data was equally divided into training and test data. The training data was labelled by hand, and on the basis of these labels appropriate feature values were recorded for each terminal category. The number of feature values recorded depended upon the representation of the category in the corpus, and this varied from over 250, for onsets and offsets, down to 120 for the "foot" categories and frication. The resulting distributions are illustrated in figures 6.5 – 6.14. The test procedure evaluates the machine performance by counting the number of correctly identified manner classes, which are themselves a part of a correctly identified utterance. A correctly identified utterance is one for which the composite degree of belief is highest, or equal highest, in the categories which exactly match a hand-labelled interpretation of the utterance.

References

Aho, A.V. and Ullman, J.D. (1972) *The theory of parsing, translation, and compiling* Vol 1, Prentice Hall.

Aho, A.V. and Peterson, T.G. (1972) A minimum distance error-correcting parser for context-free languages *SIAM J. Computing* 4

Aho, A.V., Szymanski, T.G. and Yannakakis, M. (1980) Enumerating the cartesian product of ordered sets *Proc 14th Conf. Inf. Sci. & Syst.*

Aizerman, M.A., Braverman, E.M. and Rozonoer, L.I. (1964) Theoretical foundations of the potential function method in pattern recognition *Automation and remote control* **25/6** pp821–837

Allen, J. (1985) A perspective on man-machine communication by speech *Proc IEEE* **73/11** pp1541–1500

Atal, B.S. (1983) Efficient coding of LPC parameters by temporal decomposition *Proc ICASSP–83* pp81–84

Bajpai, A.C., Calus, I. and Fairley, J.A. (1978) *Statistical methods for engineers and scientists* J.Wiley & Sons

Baker, J.K. (1975) Stochastic modelling for automatic speech understanding in Reddy, D.R. (ed), *Speech recognition* Academic Press pp521–542

Barr, A. and Feigenbaum, E.A. (1982) *The handbook of artificial intelligence* Pitman

Basilevsky, A. (1983) *Applied matrix algebra in the statistical sciences* North-Holland

Bate, E.M., Fallside, F., Gulian, E., Hinds, P. and Keiller, C. (1982) A speech training aid for the deaf with display of voicing frication and silence *Proc. ICASSP–82* pp743–746

Baum, L.E. (1972) An inequality and associated maximisation techniques in statistical estimation for probabilistic functions of a Markov process *Inequalities* **3** pp1–8

Bellman, R.E. (1957) *Dynamic Programming* Princeton University press.

Bridle, J.S. and Brown, M.D. (1979) Connected word recognition using whole word templates *Proc.Inst.Acoust.* pp25–28

Bridle, J.S. (1984) Stochastic models and template matching: some important relationships between two apparently different techniques for automatic speech recognition *Proc.Inst.Acoust.*

Brown, M.K. and Rabiner, L.R. (1982) An adaptive, ordered, graph search technique for dynamic time warping for isolated word recognition *IEEE Trans ASSP–30* pp535–544

Businger, P.A. (1965) Eigenvalues and eigenvectors of a real symmetric matrix by the QR method *Comm ACM* **8/4** pp218–219

Businger, P.A. and Golub, G.H. (1969) Singular value decomposition of a complex matrix *Comm ACM* **12** pp564–565

Buzo, A., Gray, A.H.Jr., Gray, R.M. and Markel, J.D. (1980) Speech coding based upon vector quantisation *IEEE Trans ASSP–28* pp562–574

Chien, Y.T. and Fu, K-S (1967) On the generalised Karhunen -Loéve expansion *IEEE Trans IT–13* pp518–520

Chomsky, N. (1957) *Syntactic structures* The Hague: Mouton

Chomsky, N. (1965) *Aspects of a theory of syntax* MIT Press

Chomsky, N. and Halle, M. (1968) *The sound pattern of En-*

glish New York and London, Harper and Row

Church, K.W. (1983) Phrase structure parsing: a method for taking advantage of allophonic constraints Ph.D. dissertation MIT

Cole, R.A., Rudnicky, A.I., Zue, V.W. and Reddy D.R. (1980) Speech as patterns on paper in Cole, R.A. (ed) *Perception and production of fluent speech* LEA 3-50

DeMori, R. (1983) *Computer models of speech using fuzzy algorithms* Plenum Press

Devijver, P.A. and Kittler, J. (1982) *Pattern recognition: a statistical approach* Prentice Hall

Dongarra, J., Bunch, J.R., Moler, C.B. and Stewart G.W. (1978) *LINPACK users guide* SIAM publications, Philadelphia.

Dubnowski, J., Schafer, R. and Rabiner, L.R. (1976) Realtime digital hardware pitch detector *IEEE Trans ASSP-24* 1

Duda, R.O. and Hart, P.E. (1973) *Pattern recognition and scene analysis* John Wiley

Duifhuis, H., Willems, L. and Sluyter, R. (1982) Measurement of pitch in speech: an implementation of Goldsteins theory of pitch perception *JASA* **71 6**

Earley, J. (1970) An efficient context-free parsing algorithm *Comm. ACM* **13/2**

Eckart, C. and Young, G. (1939) A principal axis transformation for non-Hermitian matrices *Bull.Amer.Math.Soc.* **45** pp118-121

Eimas, P.D. (1981) Infants speech and language: a look at some connections *Cognition* **10**

Faddeev, D.K. and Faddeeva, V.N. (1963) Computational methods of linear algebra Freeman press

Fant, C.G.M. (1973) *Speech sounds and features* MIT Press

Fisher, R.A. (1936) The use of multiple measurements in taxonomic problems *Ann. Eugenics* **7** pp179–188

Foley, D.H. and Sammon, J.W.Jr. (1975) An optimal set of discriminant vectors *IEEE Trans* C–**24** pp281–289

Forsythe, G.E. and Henrici, P. (1960) The cyclic Jacobi method for computing the principal values of a complex matrix *Proc. Amer. Math. Soc.* **94** pp1–23

Fu, K-S. and Booth, T.L. (1975) Grammatical inference introduction and survey *IEEE Trans* SMC–**5** (Jan, July)

Fu, K-S (1980) *Digital pattern recognition* Springer Verlag

Fu, K-S. and Yu T.S. (1980) *Statistical pattern classification using contextual information* Research Studies Press

Fu, K-S. (1982) *Syntactic pattern recognition and applications* Prentice Hall

Fukunaga, K. and Mantock, J.M. (1983) Non-parametric discriminant analysis *IEEE Trans* PAMI–**5** pp671–678

Galunov, V.I. and Chistovich, L.A. (1966) Relationship of motor theory to the general problem of speech recognition *Soviet Phys.Acoust.* **11** pp357–365

Gazdar, G. (1982) Phrase structure grammar in Jacobson and Pullum (eds) *The nature of syntactic representation* D.Reidel Pub.Co. pp131–186

Gimson, A.C. (1984) *An introduction to the pronounciation of English* Edward Arnold

Gold, B.and Rabiner, L.R. (1969) Parallel processing techniques for estimating pitch periods of speech in the time domain *J. Acoust. Soc. Am.* **46** pp442–449

Golub, G.H. and Van Loan, C.F. (1983) *Matrix computations* North Oxford Academic Press

Haimi-Cohen, R. and Cohen, A. (1987) Gradient-type algorithms for partial singular value decomposition *IEEE Trans* PAMI–**9** pp137–142

Harris, Z.S. (1951) *Methods in structural linguistics* University of Chicago Press

Hinton, G.E., Sejnowski, T.J. and Ackley D.H. (1984) Boltzmann machines: constraint satisfaction networks that learn *Tech Report* **CMU-CS-84-119** Carnegie-Mellon University

Ho, Y.C. and Kashyap, R.L. (1965) An algorithm for linear inequalities and its applications *IEEE Trans EC*–14/5 pp683–688

Horn, R.A. and Johnson, C.A. (1985) *Matrix analysis* Cambridge University press

Huttenlocher, D.P. and Zue, V.W. (1984) A model of lexical access based on partial phonetic information *Proc ICASSP–84*

Itakura, F. (1975) Minimum prediction residual principle applied to speech recognition *IEEE Trans ASSP*–**23** pp67–72

Jakobson, R., Fant, G. and Halle M. (1952) *Preliminaries to speech analysis: the distinctive features and their correlates* MIT press

Jelinek, F. (1976) Continuous speech recognition by statistical methods *Proc IEEE* **64** pp532–556

Joshi, A. and Levy, L. (1982) Phrase structure trees bear more fruit than you would have thought *Am.J.Comp.Ling.* **8/1**

Juang, B.H. (1984) On hidden Markov model and dynamic time warping for speech recognition - a unified view *AT&T Bell Syst. Tech. J.* **63/7** pp1213–1243

Kahn, D. (1968) Syllable-based generalisations of English phonology PhD dissertation, MIT

Kandell, A. (1982) *Fuzzy techniques in pattern recognition* John Wiley & Sons

Kendall, M.G. (1975) *Multivariate analysis* Charles Griffin & Co.Ltd

Klatt, D.H. (1976) Linguistic uses of segmental duration in English: acoustic and perceptual evidence
J. Acoust. Soc. Am., **59** pp1208–1221

Klatt, D.H. (1977) Review of the ARPA speech understanding project *J.Acoust.Soc.Am.* **62/6** pp1345–1366

Klatt, D.H. (1980) Speech perception: a model of acoustic phonetic analysis and lexical access in Cole, R.A. (ed) *Perception and production of fluent speech* LEA

Knorr, S.G. (1979) Reliable voiced/unvoiced decision *IEEE Trans ASSP–27* pp263–267

Kohonen, T., Németh, G., Bry, K-J., Jalanko, M.and Riittinen H. (1979) Spectral classification of phonemes by learning subspaces *Proc ICASSP–79* pp97–100

Kozhevnikov, V.A. and Chistovich, L.A. (1978) The nature of auditory cues in a speech signal *Soviet Phys. Acoust.* **24** 90

Ladefoged, P. (1982) *A course in phonetics* Harcourt Brace Jovanovitch

Lasry, M.J.and Stern, R.M. (1984) A posteriori estimation of correlated jointly Gaussian mean vectors
IEEE Trans PAMI–6 pp530–535

Lea, W.A. (1980) *Trends in speech recognition* Prentice Hall

Lee, H.C. and Fu, K-S. (1972) A syntactic pattern recognition system with learning capability in Tou, J.T. (ed) *Information Systems*

Levinson, S.E., Rabiner, L.R. and Sondhi M.M. (1983) An introduction to the application of the theory of probabilistic functions of a Markov process to automatic speech recognition *Bell Syst. Tech. J.* **62** pp1035–1074

Levinson, S.E. (1985a) A unified theory of composite pattern analysis for automatic speech recognition in Fallside, F.and Woods, W. (eds) *Computer speech processing* Prentice Hall

Levinson, S.E. (1985b) Structural methods in automatic speech recognition *Proc IEEE* **73/11** pp1625–1650

Lisker, L. (1985) The persuit of invariance in speech signals *J. Acoust. Soc. Am.* **77/3** pp1199–1204

Lowerre, B. (1976) The HARPY speech recognition system PhD dissertation, CMU

Lu, S.Y. and Fu, K-S (1977) Stochastic error-correcting syntax analysis for the recognition of noisy patterns *IEEE Trans* **C–26**

Lyon, R. (1982) A computational model of filtering, detection, and compression in the cochlea *Proc ICASSP–82* pp1282–1285

Markel, J.D. (1972) The SIFT algorithm for fundamental frequency estimation *IEEE Trans AU–20* 5

Markel, J.D. and Gray, A.H. (1976) *Linear Prediction of Speech* Springer-Verlag

Marr, D. (1982) *Vision* Freeman Press

Marslen-Wilson, W.D. and Tyler, L.K. (1981) Central processes in speech understanding *Phil.Trans.R.Soc.London B* **295** pp317–332

Martin, T.B. (1976) Practical applications of voice input to machines *Proc IEEE* **64** pp487–500

McCandless, S.S. (1974) An algorithm for automatic formant extraction using linear prediction spectra *IEEE Trans ASSP–22* pp135–141

Mermelstein, P. (1982) Computer recognition of continuous speech in Suen, C.Y. and DeMori, R. (eds) *Computer analysis and perception* pp81–100

Morrison, D.F. (1978) *Multivariate statistical methods* McGraw Hill

Nearey, T.M. (1978) Phonetic feature systems for vowels. Indiana University linguistics club

Nillson, N.J. (1965) *Learning machines* McGraw Hill

Oja, E. (1983) *Subspace methods of pattern recognition* Research Studies Press

Oshika and Zue, V.W. (1975) The role of phonological rules in speech understanding research *IEEE Trans ASSP*-**23** pp104–112

Pal, S.K. and Majumdar, D.D. (1977) Fuzzy sets and decision making approaches in vowel and speaker recognition *IEEE Trans SMC*-**7** pp625–629

Parzen, E. (1962) On estimation of a probability density function and mode *Ann. Math. Stat* **33** pp1065–1076

Pavlidis, T. (1978) Algorithms for shape analysis of contours and waveforms *Proc 4th Int. Conf. Pattern Recognition* pp7–10

Periera, F.C.N. and Warren, D.H.D. (1977) Definite clause grammars compared with augmented transition networks. Research report No.58, dept. AI, University of Edinburgh

Pisoni, D.B., Nusbaum, H.C., Luce, P.A. and Slowiaczek L.M. (1985) Speech perception, word recognition and the structure of the lexicon *Speech Comm.* 4 pp75–95

Poritz, A.B. (1982) Linear predictive hidden Markov models and the speech signal *Proc ICASSP*-**82** pp1291–1294

Porter, R.J. and Lubker, J.F. (1980) Rapid reproduction of vowel vowel sequences: evidence for a fast and direct acoustic-motoric linkage in speech *J.Speech Hearing Res.* **23** pp593–602

Rabiner, L.R.and Schafer, R.W. (1978) *Digital processing of speech signals* Prentice Hall

Rabiner, L.R. and Levinson, S.E. (1981) Isolated and connected word recognition - theory and selected applications *IEEE Trans COM*-**29** (May)

Rabiner, L.R., Bergh, A. and Wilpon, J. (1982) An improved

training procedure for connected digit recognition *Bell Syst. Tech. J* **61** pp681–1001

Rabiner, L.R., Levinson, S.E. and Sondhi M. (1983) On the application of vector quantization and hidden Markov models to speaker-independent isolated word recognition *Bell Syst. Tech. J* **62** (April)

Rabiner, L.R., Juang, B.H., Levinson, S.E. and Sondhi M. (1985) Some properties of continuous hidden Markov model representations *AT&T Bell Syst. Tech. J.* **64/1** pp1251–1270

Reddy, D.R. (1976) Speech recognition by machine: a review *Proc IEEE* pp501–529

Robins, H. (1948) Mixtures of distributions *Ann. Math. Stat* **19** pp360–369

Robins, H. and Monro, S. (1951) A stochastic approximation method *Annals of math. stat.* **22** pp400–407

Rosenblatt, F. (1961) *Principles of neurodynamics: perceptrons and the theory of brain mechanisms* Spartan books, Washington DC

Rosenfeld, A. and Kak, A.C. (1976) *Digital picture processing* Academic Press

Rumelhart, D.E. and McClelland, J.L. (1986) *Parallel distributed processing* MIT Press

Sears, A. (1985) DARPA speech recognition program. IEEE ASSP Workshop, Arden House, Harriman, New York

Seber, G.A.F. (1984) *Multivariate observations* John Wiley & Son

Seneff, S. (1985) Pitch and spectral analysis of speech based on an auditory synchrony model. Technical report **504** Massachusetts Institute of Technology (January)

Shipman, D.W. and Zue, V.W. (1982) Properties of large lexicons: implications for advanced isolated word recognition systems *Proc ICASSP–82* pp546–549

Smith, A.R. and Erman, L.D. (1981) NOAH - a bottom-up word hypothesizer for large vocabulary speech understanding systems *IEEE Trans PAMI-3* pp41–51

Smith, B.T., Boyle, J.M., Ikebe, Y., Klema, V.C. and Moler C.B. (1970) *Matrix eigensystem routines: EISPACK guide* Springer-Verlag.

Späth, H. (1982) *Cluster analysis algorithms* Ellis Horwood

Stevens, K.N. and Blumstein S.E. (1981) The search for invariant acoustic correlates of phonetic features in Eimas, P.D. and Millar, J.L. (eds) *Perspectives in the study of speech* LEA

Stewart, G.W. (1973) *Introduction to matrix computations* Academic Press

Strang, G. (1980) *Linear algebra and its applications* Academic Press

Tou, J.T. and Gonzalez, R.C. (1974) *Pattern recognition principles* Addison Wesley

Viterbi, A.J. (1967) Error bounds for convolutional codes and an assymptotically optimal decoding algorithm *IEEE Trans IT-13* pp260–269

Warren, D.H.D. and Pereira, F.C.N. (1977) PROLOG - the language and its implementation compared with LISP *Sigplan Notices* 12 pp109–115

Wathen-Dunn, W. (1967) *Models for the perception of speech and visual form* MIT Press

Wilkinson, J.H. and Reinsch, C. (1971) *Handbook of automatic computation, Vol 2, linear algebra* Springer Verlag

Wilpon, J.G. and Rabiner, L.R. (1985) A modified K-Means clustering algorithm for use in isolated word recognition *IEEE Trans ASSP-33* pp587–594

Winograd, T. (1983) *Language as a cognitive process* Addison Wesley

Winston, P.H. (1984) *Artificial Intelligence* Addison Wesley

Wise, J. (1955) The autocorrelation function and the spectral density function *Biometrica* **42** pp151–159

Witkin, A.P. (1983) Scale-space filtering *Proc IJCAI* pp1019–1022

Zadeh, L.A. (1975) Calculus of fuzzy restrictions. In Zadeh L.A., Fu, K-S., Tanaka, K. and Shimura, M. (eds) *Fuzzy sets and their application to cognitive decision processes* Academic Press

Zue, V.W. (1985) The use of speech knowledge in automatic speech recognition *Proc IEEE* **73/11** pp1602–1616

Index

Index

ML

This book is to be returned on or before
the last date stamped below.

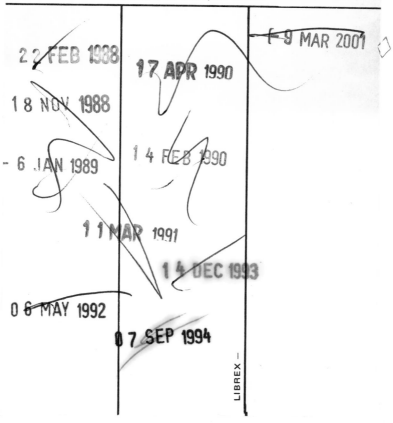

2 2 FEB 1988

1 8 NOV 1988

- 6 JAN 1989

0 6 MAY 1992

1 7 APR 1990

1 4 FEB 1990

1 1 MAR 1991

0 7 SEP 1994

1 4 DEC 1993

- 9 MAR 2001

LIBREX —